Praise for the third edition of *Managers as Mentors*

"*Managers as Mentors* is the must-read for leaders who value innovation, growth, and progress—all treasured by-products of those learning organizations where leaders mine talent."
—**Vijay Govindarajan, coauthor of the *New York Times* bestseller *Reverse Innovation* and Professor of International Business, Tuck School of Business, Dartmouth University**

"Companies today tell their managers 'You need to mentor.' Often left hanging is the question of *how*. Chip Bell and Marshall Goldsmith fill in the blanks by offering a user-friendly handbook that shows busy managers how to effectively mentor their people. Essential and full of practical wisdom."
—**Sally Helgesen, author of *The Female Advantage* and *The Web of Inclusion* and coauthor of *The Female Vision***

"*Managers as Mentors* outlines simple, easy-to-follow steps so that the mentoring role becomes comfortable and doable—even for the busiest managers."
—**Beverly Kaye, coauthor of *Help Them Grow or Watch Them Go* and the international bestseller *Love 'Em or Lose 'Em***

"As captain of the 'best damn ship in the US Navy,' I learned that the high-performance sailors typically had effective mentors. Wish I'd had this book then! I'd have given a copy to all my leaders."
—**Mike Abrashoff, author of the *New York Times* bestseller *It's Your Ship***

"The concept of this book's brilliance is that every leader must become a mentor to his or her employees. Buy the book and find out how."
—**Jeffrey Gittomer, author of the *New York Times* bestsellers *The Little Gold Book of YES! Attitude* and *The Little Red Book of Selling***

"A good manager makes you want to do a better job; a great manager makes you want to be a better person. This book will help you become the mentor you always wanted and honor the terrific ones you had."
—**Mark Goulston, author of the international bestseller *Just Listen* and coauthor of *Real Influence***

"The single most important action you can take to advance your career is to partner with a great mentor. Imagine how far you could go with two great mentors. In *Managers as Mentors*, renowned leadership experts Chip Bell and Marshall Goldsmith serve as sage mentors as you learn how to be a great one yourself."
—**Bill Treasurer, author of *Leaders Open Doors* and *Courage Goes to Work***

"*Managers as Mentors* doesn't miss a beat and only gets better with time. This third edition, structured around the SAGE model, is sage in the wisdom, experience, and stories it imparts to new and experienced mentors alike."
—**Dr. Lois J. Zachary, author of *The Mentor's Guide*, *The Mentee's Guide*, and *Creating a Mentoring Culture***

"*Managers as Mentors* provides the framework for developing emerging mentors and passing on the torch of leadership from person to person, one relationship at a time."
   —**Marianna Grachek, President and CEO, American College of Health Care Administrators**

"In the movies (and books), rarely is the remake as good as the original. That is not the case here! Take an important topic and add two brilliant and respected practitioners and what you get is this book. I read the first edition and loved it. Now, this revised third edition with illuminating additions is better than ever. If you want to help individuals (and your organization) reach anything close to their potential, read and apply this book. Start with yourself, and then share it widely. Thanks, Chip and Marshall, for a valuable addition to the learning leaders' library."
   —**Kevin Eikenberry, author of *Remarkable Leadership***

"I can't imagine any two people on this planet better equipped to take on this subject than Marshall and Chip. For those seeking advice in building successful mentoring partnerships, this is your book."
   —**Gordon Peters, Founding Chairman and CEO, Institute for Management Studies**

"The book managers everywhere have been waiting for: a clear and practical guide to tapping talent in their organizations. If you ever wondered what managers in 'learning organizations' are supposed to be doing, here's your answer."
   —**Nancy K. Austin, coauthor (with Tom Peters) of *A Passion for Excellence***

"Continual learning is a key to effective leadership because no one can know everything there is to know. *Managers as Mentors* is a practical yet powerful book for helping leaders make continual learning a valuable addition to their strategy."
   —**Mike Krzyzewski, Head Coach, Duke University Men's Basketball, 2010 NCAA Champions**

"Mentoring is the highest of the teaching arts, and in this new edition of *Managers as Mentors* Chip Bell and Marshall Goldsmith have skillfully crafted the essential handbook for all those who are trusted advisors to aspiring leaders."
   —**Jim Kouzes, coauthor, *The Leadership Challenge* and Executive Fellow of Leadership, Leavey School of Business, Santa Clara University**

"*Managers as Mentors* will be the indispensable handbook of managers/leaders across the sectors."
   —**Frances Hesselbein, President and CEO, The Frances Hesselbein Leadership Institute and former CEO of the Girls Scouts of the USA**

managers as
Mentors

THIRD EDITION, REVISED AND EXPANDED

managers as Mentors

Building Partnerships for Learning

CHIP R. BELL AND MARSHALL GOLDSMITH

BK

Berrett–Koehler Publishers, Inc.
San Francisco
a BK Business book

Berrett-Koehler Publishers, Inc.
235 Montgomery Street, Suite 650
San Francisco, CA 94104-2916
Tel: (415) 288-0260 Fax: (415) 362-2512   www.bkconnection.com

Ordering Information

Quantity sales. Special discounts are available on quantity purchases by corporations, associations, and others. For details, contact the "Special Sales Department" at the Berrett-Koehler address above.

Individual sales. Berrett-Koehler publications are available through most bookstores. They can also be ordered directly from Berrett-Koehler: Tel: (800) 929-2929; Fax: (802) 864-7626; www.bkconnection.com

Orders for college textbook/course adoption use. Please contact Berrett-Koehler: Tel: (800) 929-2929; Fax: (802) 864-7626.

Orders by U.S. trade bookstores and wholesalers. Please contact Ingram Publisher Services, Tel: (800) 509-4887; Fax: (800) 838-1149; E-mail: customer.service@ingrampublisherservices.com; or visit www.ingrampublisherservices.com/Ordering for details about electronic ordering.

Berrett-Koehler and the BK logo are registered trademarks of Berrett-Koehler Publishers, Inc.

Printed in the United States of America

Berrett-Koehler books are printed on long-lasting acid-free paper. When it is available, we choose paper that has been manufactured by environmentally responsible processes. These may include using trees grown in sustainable forests, incorporating recycled paper, minimizing chlorine in bleaching, or recycling the energy produced at the paper mill.

Library of Congress Cataloging-in-Publication Data
Bell, Chip R.
Managers as mentors : building partnerships for learning / Chip R. Bell and Marshall Goldsmith. — [Third edition].
     pages cm
Includes bibliographical references and index.
ISBN 978-1-60994-710-1 (pbk.)
1. Mentoring in business. 2. Executives. 3. Employees—Training of.
4. Employees—Counseling of. I. Goldsmith, Marshall. II. Title.
HF5385.B45 2013
658.3'124—dc23
                    2013008478

Third Edition
18 17 16 15 14 13   10 9 8 7 6 5 4 3 2 1

Text design and production: Detta Penna
Developmental editor: Jamie Fuller
Copyediting: Susan Padgett
Proofreading: Katherine Lee
Index: Kirsten Kite
Cover design: Cassandra Chu

Cover image: © Kutsal Lenger iStockphoto

Contents

Beginning Our Journey

What is mentoring? At its most basic level, it is simply the act of helping another learn. However, the relationship between helper and helpee changes significantly when performed as a learning partnership rather than the traditional teaching "parentship" (master teaches apprentice).

The concept of mentoring as a learning partnership is one rather foreign to many. They rely on the stereotypical approach, using their expertise to teach rather than facilitate; demonstrate instead of enabling discovery. Lecturing to their protégés, they leave them temporarily capable but unwise in the long run. What comes from a capability-adding approach is only compliance; however, what emanates from a wisdom-building approach is creativity—the foundation of innovation. Competitive organizations today need "learning entrepreneurs." Today, curiosity almost always trumps conformity.

Words like "mentor" and "coach" are sometimes used to mean the same thing. Here is our distinction: Coaching is a part of the leadership role specifically aimed at nurturing and sustaining performance. Mentoring is that part of the leadership role that has learning (competence, proficiency, skill, know-how, wisdom) as its primary outcome. Granted, learning impacts performance, and that in turn impacts the accomplishment of important goals. You will encounter this definition more than once.

The words we use for the players in the mentoring partnership are chosen more for convenience than for any other reason. "Mentors" are people (especially leaders) who engage in deliberate actions aimed at promoting learning; "leader," "manager," or "coach" would serve as well. Mentors do not have to be in a superior power position. One might easily be mentored by someone who possesses the needed skill or competence but is several levels below in the pecking order.

Some organizations find the label "mentor" to have special negative baggage, often the result of ill-fated mentoring programs. "Learning coach" is often a solid substitute. Likewise, "protégé" refers to the primary beneficiary of the mentoring effort; "associate," "subordinate," "colleague," "mentee," "partner," or "follower" could be used. As long as we are clear on whom we mean, the labels can be changed to fit individual preferences and situations.

The main thing to remember is that this book is grounded in a partnership philosophy. It has no secrets aimed at making you look good to an unknowing subordinate, and we hope you will share it with your colleagues and associates and protégés. The more you know about how to mentor, the better the mentoring relationship will work for you. The same is true for the protégé. Some have found discussing the book helpful in improving the process of mentoring. Do what works for you.

Managers As Mentors, ReVISITED

We are big fans of new. We rarely go to the same restaurant twice, even if it was a great experience. The concept of a time-share—returning each summer to the same condo—leaves us absolutely cold. Why, we won't even eat leftovers unless the only other option is to skip a meal!

This is the third edition of this book. You would think we would abhor the idea of spending time on the "leftover" version of a book. But we were excited by the opportunity! This edition is not a warmed-over version of yesterday's dish, served up with a different sauce on the side. We think you'll discover it has enough new and different ingredients not to be considered a leftover at all; rather, it is a completely new experience.

This new version is different in a number of ways. There are many chapters in this edition not found in the first or second. We have learned a lot both from the feedback of readers of the second edition and from participants in the mentoring workshops we have conducted and keynote speeches we have delivered. They helped us crystallize our thinking and enabled us to get a lot clearer on concepts that were somewhat vague in the second edition. We are grateful for the learning they provided us.

You will discover soon that *Managers as Mentors* is crafted around a mnemonic—SAGE—that forms the structure of the mentoring experience as we see it. *Surrendering* (S) is all about actions that make mentoring a power-free experience. We have learned that power, authority, and command—or at least the protégé's perception of these traits in the mentor—can doom the mentoring experience to a perfunctory dialogue ... sans risks, sans spirit, and sans discovery.

Accepting (A) in the SAGE model focuses on the value of a safe, nontoxic relationship. When the protégé believes he or she is in a relationship that is not dangerous, growth-producing risk and experimentation are more likely to occur. The perception or prediction of danger is related not to physical harm but rather to the emotional damage caused by rebuke, judgment, or criticism—all of which yield a loss of protégé self-esteem in front of an important person. Why is this important? Without risk there is no learning; without experimentation there is no progress.

Gifting (G) is positioned as the main event in mentoring. Many mentors start their mentoring relationships with a gift of advice, feedback, or focus. However, when offered as the first step in the relationship, the act of bestowing such gifts risks their being at best undervalued, at worst ignored, resisted, or rejected. If Gifting follows Surrendering and Accepting, it is more likely to be experienced by the protégé as a sincere gesture and a valued contribution worthy of attention, tryout, and effort.

Extending (E) in the SAGE is about the creation and nurturance of the protégé as a self-directed learner. It is also about ways to extend the learning of the protégé beyond his or her relationship with the mentor. Essentially, it is shepherding the transfer of learning.

Why Mentoring Is Important ... Today

Organizations scramble to attract and retain skilled employees. Mentoring can be a powerful weapon useful in winning the war for talent. And both the flattening of organizations and the transformation of the role of boss have left many managers in an identity crisis. Having risen up the hierarchy by virtue of their command and control skills, they enter a world where bossing is now about coaching and partnering. This book offers a new perspective on roles and competencies for bosses as an alternative to what it has meant historically to be in charge.

Organizations have always operated in a competitive arena. Whether vying for a share of an economic market, a share of the customer's loyalty, or a share of the resources doled out by some governing body, organizations operate in a contest mode. In today's race, the winners are those that prove themselves more adaptive, more innovative, and more agile. These are the organizations populated by employees who are always learning, led by managers who are always teaching. So at a macro level, this book is about achieving organizational success.

When *Managers as Mentors* first came out, the concept of the "learning organization" was new and popular. Peter Senge was the new management guru, and his groundbreaking best-seller, *The Fifth Discipline,* was required reading for all contemporary, forward-thinking executives. We have today moved past the fad stage of a learning organization.[1] The landscape of enterprise now is shaped by the dearth of talent, the pace of change, and the transformation of what it means to be in charge—all operating against the backdrop of a challenging economy. This new landscape has put "helping employees grow" at the top of the list of critical success factors for all managers. Consequently, this book is more important today than it was when it first appeared in hardback in the fall of 1996.

As mentoring has grown in importance since then, so have the specifications for mentoring tools. Managers today want proficiency without having to buy into a program. They seek helpful resources and techniques, not hindering rules and policies. Explorations of philosophy and theory might be tolerated after hours, but in the middle of challenge and the heat of contest, managers shun any instruction not immediately transferable to their everyday practice.

Mentoring as an Art

The mentor is a teacher, a guide, a sage, and foremost a person acting to the best of his or her ability, in a whole and compassionate way in plain view of the protégé. No greater helping or healing can occur than that induced by a model of compassion and authenticity. Mentoring is about being real, being a catalyst, and being sometimes a kind of prophet. It is therefore far more art than science. It is about personal power, not expert or role power. The most powerful and most difficult part of mentoring is being who you are.

This is not to imply that a mentor must be some kind of super-hero without flaws, doubts, or the capacity for making mistakes. Fundamentally, mentoring is about growing—mentors growing with protégés, protégés growing with mentors. The core of a mentoring relationship is more about a mutual search than about imparting wisdom. As a collective pursuit, mentoring works best when mentors are focused on building, not on boasting.

The anthropologist Carlos Castaneda used the word "magic" to describe his unique mentoring relationship with the Yaqui medicine man Don Juan—and truly there is a magical quality to the mentoring process when it takes on a life of its own and leads mentor and protégé through an experience of shared discovery.[2] The challenge of helping another see things in a new way has had many labels down through the centuries. Biblical writers used fishing analogies to capture the spirit of mentoring magic and told of removing scales from eyes. The philosopher Ram Dass referred to it as "a dance."[3] Buddha said, "One should follow a man of wisdom who rebukes one for one's faults, as one would follow a guide to some buried treasure."

Mentoring magic cannot be a solo performance. It is not a one-way, master-to-novice transaction. To be effective and lasting, it must be accomplished through a two-way relationship—the synchronized efforts of two people. The synchrony and synergy of mentoring are what give it a dance-like quality. They are also what make it magical.

This is not the first book on mentoring—nor the last. But from what we have seen, it is the only one we know of that is grounded in a true partnership philosophy. Our take on mentoring with a partnership philosophy is this: assume that all your future employees will be independently wealthy, headstrong, purpose-seeking volunteers who love to acquire learning but hate to surrender liberty.

This book is also about power-free facilitation of learning. It is about teaching through the power of consultation and collaboration rather than constriction and assessment. It views learning as an expansive, unfolding process rather than an evaluative, narrowing effort. It is a song about unfolding—one in which the last few stanzas have yet to be written. It is the instruction book on how to perform synchronized magic.

This is not a philosophy book, although it is grounded in very specific convictions: that the principal goal of mentoring is to create a self-directed learner, that the primary tool for learning is discovery, and that the most effective context for reaching that goal is a learning partnership. This is a workbook, filled with ideas, suggestions, how-to's, and resources. If it ends up dog-eared, underlined, and passed around, it will mean that we have succeeded in making it a practical book—perhaps even a fun book as well as a soul-searching one. It is intended to be a tool for a critical component of the leader's responsibility—helping another learn and grow.

We wanted you to have a preview of coming attractions. Below are thumbnails showing the organization of the book.

Part 1: Mentoring Is...

Chapter 1: Panning for Insight: The Art of Mentoring outlines what mentoring is (and is not), describes mentoring traps to avoid, and offers perspectives on how to make the mentoring relationship effective. This chapter also provides an overview of the mentoring model used to structure the book.

Chapter 2: Mentoring in Action: The Act of Mentoring Up Close has a simple and singular purpose: to present the feel and drama of mentoring. Often participants in coaching and mentoring classes ask, "Could you show a movie of what solid mentoring looks like, so we could know it when we see it?" This chapter attempts to provide the screenplay for such a movie. It will be a case to which we return throughout the book to make key points about the mentoring partnership.

Chapter 3: Assessing Your Mentoring Talents: A Self-Check Scale is the chapter with the self-scoring instrument. Since several chapters have sidebars that apply the results of this instrument, we recommend that you read this chapter and do the self-check before going on to other chapters. Read chapters 1 through 3 first, then select whatever chapter fits your need. You are welcome to photocopy the instrument if you would rather not write in the book.

Chapter 4: Case Study: Every Knock's a Boost. Throughout this edition of *Managers as Mentors*, we provide case examples of well-known leaders describing their experiences as the protégés to effective mentors. The first case study is an interview with Mark Tercek, CEO of The Nature Conservancy. The Nature Conservancy is the leading conservation organization working around the world to protect ecologically important lands and waters for nature and people. Before joining The Nature Conservancy, Mark was a managing director at Goldman Sachs, where he played a key role in developing the firm's environmental strategy. He holds an MBA from the Harvard Business School.

Part 2: Surrendering—Leveling the Learning Field

Chapter 5: Kindling Kinship: The Power of Rapport makes the point that the way the mentoring relationship begins can strongly influence how effective it will be later. This chapter provides both perspectives and techniques for getting the mentoring relationship off to a solid start.

Chapter 6: The Elements of Trust Making: "This Could Be the Start of Something Big!" shows how the quality of the mentoring relationship hangs on the success the mentor has in nurturing, communicating, and engendering trust. Using the style of the late great comedian Steve Allen as a prototype, the chapter outlines practices important to trust building.

Chapter 7: The Person in the Mirror: Mentor Humility Creates Protégé Confidence focuses on ways to narrow the emotional distance between mentor and protégé. This chapter, written exclusively by Marshall, outlines power-reducing techniques to create a level playing field for a mentoring relationship to be productive.

Chapter 8: Inside the Mind of the Protégé: When Fear and Learning Collide. One of the greatest barriers to learning is fear. Most leader-follower relationships have some element of anxiety, given the ever-present existence of position power (in the case of a boss) or expertise (in the case of a peer) or both. Likewise, most organizations still spend a lot of energy on evaluation, testing, and judging—all potential anxiety producers. This chapter examines ways to make a mentoring relationship a safe haven from apprehension for the protégé, thus a healthy environment for learning.

Chapter 9: Case Study: Fail Faster. This chapter offers an interview with Liz Smith, CEO of Bloomin' Brands. Bloomin' Brands is one of the world's largest casual dining companies, with more than 1,400 restaurants in forty-nine states and twenty-one countries and territories. The company owns such familiar brands as Outback Steakhouse, Bonefish Grill, and Carrabba's Italian Grill. Before assuming leadership at Bloomin' Brands, Ms. Smith was president of Avon Products, Inc. She holds an MBA from Stanford University.

Part 3: Accepting—Creating a Safe Haven for Risk Taking

Chapter 10: Invitations to Risk: Acceptance as a Nurturer of Courage. The process of moving from novice to mastery is clear. The protégé must embrace the risk of making errors and even ending in failure. To take such a risk, particularly in the presence of another, requires courage. And it is thus a key task of a mentor to communicate the kind of acceptance that will create a safe environment in which the protégé can experiment.

Chapter 11: Socrates' Great Secret: Awesome Queries focuses on the power of asking questions that foster a protégé's feeling of acceptance. Fair-weather questions at a family reunion, for instance, leave you with a very different feeling than do the questions that demonstrate sincere curiosity. Everyone knows how to ask questions, but good mentoring uses inquiry as a tool to enrich the relationship while facilitating insight and discovery. Mastering the techniques in this chapter can benefit all interpersonal relationships.

Chapter 12: The Ear of an Ally: The Lost Art of Listening focuses on the importance and power of cultivating acceptance through listening. The initial temptation may be to skip this chapter, saying to yourself, "I know how to listen!" Try to resist. Readers of previous editions indicated that this chapter may be the most powerful one in the book because it offers a much deeper and richer definition of listening than generally discussed in how-to communication books.

Chapter 13: "Give-and-Take" Starts with "Give": Distinguished Dialogues is not a chapter about questions and answers. Rather, it offers interpersonal tools on how to make a discussion more of an insightful (full of insight) conversation. This chapter takes Socrates' secret (chapter 11) to an advanced level of application, complete with techniques for restarting a stalled or sidetracked discussion or stopping a discussion that has become unproductive.

Chapter 14: Case Study: Simply Listen. This is an interview with Deanna Mulligan, CEO of the Guardian Life Insurance Company of America. The Guardian Life Insurance Company of America is a Fortune 300 company founded in 1860 and the fourth-largest mutual life insurance company in the United States. Prior to joining Guardian in 2008, Ms. Mulligan was founding partner of DMM Management Solutions, LLC, a life insurance consultancy. She was a principal at McKinsey and Company, where she additionally served as co-leader of the North American Life Insurance Practice. Ms. Mulligan holds an MBA from Stanford University. She was listed by *Fortune* as one of the 50 most powerful women in U.S. business.

Part 4: Gifting—The Main Event

Chapter 15: Avoiding Thin Ice: The Gift of *Advice*. Most people think the main thing mentors do is give advice. But if done inappropriately, advice giving is one of the most dangerous actions a mentor can take. This chapter provides techniques for giving advice while minimizing resistance.

Chapter 16: Reporting on Blind Spots: The Gifts of *Feedback* and *Feedforward*. While advice is tricky to deliver without prompting protégé resistance, giving feedback is even more difficult. The by-product of advice poorly given is resistance, the reluctance of the protégé to value the information. However, the by-product of feedback inadequately delivered is resentment, a sense of bitterness on the part of the protégé that the mentor has a perspective unattainable by the protégé. Chapter 17 focuses on ways to make your comments count.

Chapter 17: Linking Proficiency to Purpose: The Gift of *Focus* makes the point that adult learning must have a sense of rationale if it is to ensure the protégé's motivation and interest. This chapter outlines several approaches to anchoring learning in a fashion that guarantees relevance and purpose.

Chapter 18: The Bluebirds' Secret: The Gift of *Balance* explores the role of balance in fostering growth. One of a mentor's most challenging dilemmas is to find a balance between providing guidance and giving the protégé freedom. The "when to hold 'em, when to fold 'em" challenge is especially tricky as the protégé approaches competence and independence. This chapter is written exclusively by Chip.

Chapter 19: Inviting Your Protégé to Enchantment: The Gift of *Story* acknowledges the power of storytelling as a teaching tool. Most people count a parent, grandparent, or elementary school teacher as their earliest mentoring relationship. Lessons learned at an elder's knee were often laced with a "Let me tell you about the time I…" instructive tale. Whether labeled a parable, anecdote, fable, or yarn, stories can foster insight and discovery like no other tool.

Chapter 20: Case Study: Grace under Fire. This is an interview with Joe Almeida, CEO of Covidien. Covidien is a global healthcare products leader dedicated to innovative medical solutions for better patient outcomes. It has a market cap of over $26 billion. Before joining Covidien, Mr. Almeida was a director of manufacturing in American Home Products' Acufex Microsurgical division, an engineering manager of Johnson & Johnson's Professional Products division, and a management consultant at Andersen Consulting (now Accenture). Mr. Almeida holds a bachelor's degree from Escola de Engenharia Maua in São Paulo, Brazil.

Part 5: Extending—Nurturing a Self-Directed Learner

Chapter 21: Beyond the Relationship: Ensuring the Transfer of Learning. The mentor's responsibility for the partnership does not end at the outer edge of the relationship. Successful mentors must look to ensure that what is learned makes a difference. This means remaining ever vigilant for barriers and obstacles that diminish the efficient transfer of learning.

Chapter 22: "If You Want Something to Grow, Pour Champagne on It!" A key part of the mentor's role and responsibility is to provide affirmation to their protégé. Affirming is more than a pat on the back. It includes advocating for the protégé, valuing their achievements as well as their effort, and anchoring their nurturance to a larger vision.

Chapter 23: Managing Sweet Sorrow: Life after Mentoring. Almost every mentoring relationship eventually comes to an end. The protégé outgrows the wisdom of the mentor; the protégé's learning needs shift to an area requiring a different mentor; the protégé or the mentor moves to a new role or place. How the relationship ends affects the readiness of both to establish new mentoring relationships. The parting is a potent platform for continuing growth.

Chapter 24: Case Study: Fly High, Dive Deep. This is an interview with Fred Hassan, managing director of Warburg Pincus, LLC. Warburg Pincus, LLC, is a global private equity firm with offices in the United States, Europe, Brazil, China, and India. Established more than forty years ago, Warburg Pincus has invested more than $40 billion in over 650 companies in more than thirty countries around the world. Mr. Hassan, a native of Pakistan, was chairman of the board of Bausch & Lomb. Prior to that, he was CEO of Schering-Plough from 2003 until late 2009. He holds an MBA from the Harvard Business School.

Part 6: Special Conditions

Chapter 25: Unholy Alliances: Mentoring in Precarious Relationships. Most of this book is concerned with traditional mentoring relationships. This chapter examines some unique ones. Starting with mentoring situations in which mentor and protégé are equal—that is, peers—the chapter offers insight to situations in which mentor and protégé are enough "different" to potentially impact how the relationship is managed.

Chapter 26: Arduous Alliances: Mentoring in Precarious Situations. As relationships can be precarious, so can situations. This chapter looks at three unique complexities: mentoring in today's

"Time's up!" fast-paced work world, mentoring when protégé and mentor work in different places or have only intermittent contact, and mentoring with the assistance of technology.

Chapter 27: Case Study: Respect Everyone. Our final interview is with Frances Hesselbein, CEO of the Frances Hesselbein Leadership Institute. Established in 1990 as the Peter F. Drucker Foundation for Nonprofit Management, the Frances Hesselbein Leadership Institute furthers its mission to strengthen and inspire the leadership of the social sector and their partners in business and government by connecting the public, private, and social sectors with curated resources and relationships to serve, evolve, and lead together. Ms. Hesselbein served as the CEO for the Girl Scouts of the USA between 1976 and 1990. She is a winner of the Presidential Medal of Freedom (the highest award that can be given to a U.S. civilian) and is the recipient of twenty honorary doctoral degrees.

Part 7: The Mentor's Toolkit

Tool #1: Quick Tips for Mentors and Protégés is the one part of the book in which we offer suggestions for the protégé as well as the mentor. Think of this as your mentoring crib sheet.

Tool #2: Mentoring Competence Measure is a short instrument that gives you a quick read on your strengths and improvement opportunities as a mentor. Be honest and you gain food for reflection.

Tool #3: Mentoring FAQs came from countless workshops we have conducted. We select the questions most frequently asked from participants about how to be a great mentor.

Tool #4: More Reading on Mentoring is a list of our favorite books on mentoring. You will find a much more extensive bibliography at the end of the book.

Tool #5: Elements of a Learning Plan offers a simple structure for a learning plan many mentor-protégé relationships have found useful in providing organization to their work. Use it, adapt it, and make it yours.

Tool #6: The Eagle is a poignant story we included for your inspiration. It reminds us to appreciate the many powerful lessons we can learn from nature around us.

How to Get the Most from This Book

Most books are written to be read from beginning to end. This is not one of them. However, you will benefit from initially reading the introduction and first section (chapters 1 through 3). Chapter 3 contains a self-scoring instrument referred to in several chapters throughout the book. To derive the greatest learning from those later chapters, complete and score this instrument first.

Before reading any chapter, start with a goal. Select a relationship you seek to improve, a skill you want to enhance, or a mentoring problem you want to solve. Choose the chapter that seems best suited to addressing that relationship, skill, or challenge. As you read the chapter, make notes on how you might apply the techniques you find.

We hope you prosper from and enjoy this book. We would very much appreciate your feedback on its usefulness, as well as your ideas on ways it might be improved in future editions. You will find our addresses at the bottom of the last page. Drop us a note or give us a call. Happy mentoring!

Chip R. Bell   *Marshall Goldsmith*
Greensboro, Georgia   *Rancho Santa Fe, California*

PART 1

MENTORING IS...

I am not a teacher, but an awakener.

Robert Frost

Take a minute to recall the people in your life who were effective at helping you learn something important. (We'll wait.) Chip's mother taught him a lot about dating etiquette when he was a teenager; one of Marshall's doctoral professors at UCLA taught him about humility. Who taught you emotional intelligence in an adult world? Where did you learn to not call the CEO by her first name, how to get a great table at a restaurant, where to put your soup spoon when you have finished your soup, or how full to fill the wineglasses when you have guests over for dinner? Over the course of our lives, learning comes from many people, in many places, and through many events.

What are the reasons that people sometimes learn and sometimes fail to learn? What are the reasons that some people are skilled at helping others with personal or professional growth and some are not? Why does mentoring sometimes make an impact and at other times seem a complete waste of time and energy?

What conditions and competencies spark discovery, insight, and understanding?

The complete answers to questions like these could occupy volumes—and you're holding only a single book. As you will see, there *are* tools, tips, tactics, and techniques that make mentoring easier to understand, more effective, and a lot more fun—but to become good at the game, we must first mark off the playing field. Before we learn the pointers, we need to be clear on the meaning of mentoring and in harmony with the conditions conducive to its effectiveness.

The goal of the next few chapters is to explain the arena or context of mentoring. We opened the book by defining mentoring as simply "the act of helping another learn." Mentoring is traditionally thought of as a transaction between a tutor and somebody else's subordinate. However, *Managers as Mentors* will focus largely on the leader mentoring a follower. This will require a unique alteration in the relationship—actions aimed at eliminating (or at least reducing) the role that position power plays in the tutelage.

The mentoring arena is filled with assumptions about how people learn, roles mentors can play, qualities mentors should pursue, and traps mentors need to avoid. Because the mentor is also a learner, the intent of the next few chapters is to prompt self-examination, to advocate clarity of mission, and to nurture the linkage of who we are with what we do.

1

Panning for Insight
The Art of Mentoring

Learning is not attained by chance; it must be sought for with ardor and attended to with diligence.

Abigail Adams (1780)

Panning for gold is a lot like mentoring. It is not always easy. Panning for gold works like this. First, you put a double handful of sand in a heavy-gauge steel shallow pan and dip it in the water, filling it half full of water. Next, you gently move the pan back and forth as you let small amounts of yellow sand wash over the side of the pan.

The objective is to let the black sand sink to the bottom of the gold pan. But this is the point where panning for gold gets real serious. Impatience or strong-arming the way the pan is shaken means 'the black sand escapes over the side along with the yellow sand. Once black sand is the only sand left in the pan, you are rewarded with flecks of gold. The gold resides among the black sand.

Mentoring can be like panning for gold among the sand. Insight is generally not lying on top ready to be found and polished. If it were easy pickings, the help of a mentor would be unnecessary. It lies beneath the obvious and ordinary. It is lodged in the dark sands of irrational beliefs, myths, fears, prejudices, and biases. It lurks under untested hunches, ill-prepared starts, and unfortunate mistakes. Helping the protégé extract insight takes patience and persistence. It cannot be rushed and haphazardly forced. And, most of all, it cannot be strong-armed with the force of the mentor. It must be discovered by the protégé with the guidance of the mentor.

As a mentor, you are in charge of getting the protégé to properly shake the pan. You help the protégé learn to recognize the real treasures of insight and understanding and not be seduced by "fool's gold"—achieved by rote and temporarily retained only "until the exam is over." The way you help the protégé handle the dark sand is central to the acquisition of wisdom. That is the essence of mentoring with a partnership philosophy.

What is the nature of your responsibility? The whole concept of mentor has had a checkered path in the world of work. The most typical mental image has been that of a seasoned corporate sage conversing with a naïve, wet-behind-the-ears young recruit. The conversation would probably have been laced with informal rules, closely guarded secrets, and "I remember back in '77 . . . " stories of daredevil heroics and too-close-to-call tactics. And work-based mentoring has had an almost heady, academic sound, reserved solely for workers in white collars whose fathers advised, "Get to know ol' Charlie."

In recent years the term "mentor" became connected less with privilege and more with affirmative action. An organization viewed as a part of its responsibility enabling minority employees through a mentor to expedite their route through glass ceilings, beyond old-boy networks and the private winks formerly reserved for WASP males. Such mentoring sponsors sometimes salved the consciences of those who bravely talked goodness but became squeamish if expected to spearhead courageous acts. These mentoring programs sounded contemporary and forward-thinking. Some were of great service, but many were just lip service.

But what are the role and responsibility of mentoring, really? When the package is unwrapped and the politically correct is scraped away, what's left? A mentor is defined in the dictionary as "a wise, trusted advisor...a teacher or coach." Such a simple definition communicates a plain-vanilla context. In case you missed the preface, mentoring is defined as that part of the leader's role that has learning as its primary outcome. Bottom line, a mentor is simply someone who helps someone else learn something that would have otherwise been learned less well, more slowly, or not at all. Notice the power-free nature of this definition; mentors are not power figures.

The traditional use of the word "mentor" denotes a person outside one's usual chain of command—from the junior's point of view, someone who "can help me understand the informal system and offer guidance on how to be successful in this crazy organization." Not all mentors are supervisors or managers, but most effective supervisors and managers act as mentors. Mentoring is typically focused on one person; group mentoring is training or teaching. We will focus on the one-to-one relationship; the others are beyond the scope of this book.

Good leaders do a lot of things in the organizations they inhabit. Good leaders communicate a clear vision and articulate a precise direction. Good leaders provide performance feedback, inspire and encourage, and, when necessary, discipline. Good leaders also mentor. Once more, mentoring is that part of a leader's role that has growth as its primary outcome.

Lessons from the First Mentor

The word "mentor" comes from *The Odyssey*, written by the Greek poet Homer. As Odysseus (Ulysses, in the Latin translation) is preparing to go fight the Trojan War, he realizes he is leaving behind his one and only heir, Telemachus. Since "Telie" (as he was probably known to his buddies) is in junior high, and since wars tended to drag on for years (the Trojan War lasted ten), Odysseus recognizes that Telie needs to be coached on how to "king" while Daddy is off fighting. He hires a trusted family friend named Mentor to be Telie's tutor. Mentor is both wise and sensitive—two important ingredients of world-class mentoring.

The history of the word "mentor" is instructive for several reasons. First, it underscores the legacy nature of mentoring. Like Odysseus, great leaders strive to leave behind a benefaction of added value. Second, Mentor (the old man) combined the wisdom of experience with the sensitivity of a fawn in his attempts to convey kinging skills to young Telemachus. We all know the challenge of conveying our hard-won wisdom to another without resistance. The successful mentor is able to circumvent resistance.

Homer characterizes Mentor as a family friend. The symbolism contained in this relationship is apropos to contemporary mentors. Effective mentors are like friends in that their goal is to create a safe context for growth. They are also like family in that their focus is to offer an unconditional, faithful acceptance of the protégé. Friends work to add and multiply, not subtract. Family members care, even in the face of mistakes and errors.

Superior mentors know how adults learn. Operating out of their intuition or on what they have learned from books, classes, or other mentors, the best mentors recognize that they are, first and foremost, facilitators and catalysts in a process of discovery and insight. They know that mentoring is not about smart comments, eloquent lectures, or clever quips. Mentors practice their skills with a combination of never-ending compassion, crystal-clear communication, and a sincere joy in the role of being a helper along a journey toward mastering.

Just like the first practitioner of their craft, mentors love learning, not teaching. They treasure sharing rather than showing off, giving rather than boasting. Great mentors are not only devoted fans of their protégés, they are loyal fans of the dream of what their protégés can become with their guidance.

Traps to Avoid

There are countless traps along the path of mentordom. Mentoring can be a power trip for those seeking an admirer, a manifestation of greed for those who must have slaves. Mentoring can be a platform for proselytizing for a cause or crusade, a strong tale told to an innocent or unknowing listener. However, the traps of power, greed, and crusading all pale when compared with the subtler "watch out fors" listed below. There are other traps, of course, but these are the ones that most frequently raise their ugly heads to sabotage healthy relationships.

Keep the traps in mind as you read the rest of the book; search for them within yourself. By the time you've read the last page, you will perhaps have learned to avoid those to which you are most susceptible.

I Can Help

When is help helpful and when is it harmful? People inclined to be charitable with their time, energy, and expertise often attempt to help when what the learner actually needs is to struggle and find her own way. Here's a test: if you ask the protégé, "May I help?" and she says no, how do you feel? Be honest with yourself. If you react with even a trace of rejection and self-pity, this may be your trap to avoid.

I Know Best

Some people become mentors because they enjoy being recognized as someone in the know. They relish the affirmations from protégés who brag to others about their helpful mentor. They especially like protégés who regularly compliment them on their contribution. This is a trap! You may get off track and end up using the protégé for your own recognition needs. The test? If your protégé comes to you and says that he has found someone else who might be more helpful as a mentor, how do you react? If you feel more than mild and momentary disappointment, beware! This may be your special trap.

I Can Help You Get Ahead

Mentors can be useful in getting around organizational barriers, getting into offices otherwise closed, and getting special tips useful in climbing the ladder of success. As sometime kingmakers, they make promises that can carry an "I can get it for you wholesale" seduction. All these "gettings" can be valuable and important. They can also add a bartering, sinister component to an otherwise promising relationship. The "You scratch my back, and ..." approach to mentoring relationships can infuse a scorekeeping dimension that is detrimental to both parties. Although reciprocity can be important, a tit-for-tat aspect can lead one person in the relationship to a scorekeeping, "You owe me one" view of the relationship.

You Need Me

When mentors feel that their protégés need them, they are laying the groundwork for a relationship based on dependence. Although many mentor-protégé partnerships begin with some degree of dependence, the goal is to transform the relationship into one of strength and interdependence. A relationship based on dependence can ultimately become a source of resentment for the protégé, false power for the mentor.

If the protégé views the mentoring process as a chore or a necessary ritual, it is generally a dependent relationship that will not be allowed to grow up. Remember, the focus should be on helping the protégé become strong, not on helping the protégé feel better about being weak.

The Qualities of Great Mentoring

Great mentors are not immune to traps; great mentors recognize the traps they are likely to fall into and work hard to compensate for them. How do they do that? They do it by understanding the qualities of a mentor-protégé relationship focused on discovery and learner independence—and then learning to be living, breathing models of those qualities.

First and foremost, great mentoring is a partnership. And partnership starts with balance.

Balance

Unlike a relationship based on power and control, a learning partnership is a balanced alliance, grounded in mutual interests, interdependence, and respect. Power-seeking mentors tend to mentor with credentials and sovereignty; partnership-driven mentors seek to mentor with authenticity and openness. In a balanced learning partnership, energy is given early in the relationship to role clarity and communication of expectations; there is a spirit of generosity and acceptance rather than a focus on rules and rights. Partners recognize their differences while respecting their common needs and objectives.

Truth

Countless books extol the benefits of clear and accurate communication. Partnership communication has one additional quality: it is clean, pure, characterized by the highest level of integrity and honesty. Truth-seekers work not only to ensure that their words are pure (the truth and nothing but the truth) but also to help others communicate with equal purity. When a mentor works hard to give feedback to a protégé in a way that is caringly frank and compassionately straightforward, it is in pursuit of clean communication. When a mentor implores the protégé for candid feedback, it is a plea for clean communication. The path of learning begins with the mentor's genuineness and candor.

Trust

Trust begins with experience; experience begins with a leap of faith. Perfect monologues, even with airtight proof and solid support documentation, do not foster a climate of experimentation and risk taking. They foster passive acceptance, not personal investment. If protégés see their mentors taking risks, they will follow suit. A "trust-full" partnership is one in which error is accepted as a necessary step on the path from novice to master.

Abundance

Partnership-driven mentors exude generosity. There is a giver orientation that finds enchantment in sharing wisdom. As the "Father of Adult Learning," Malcolm Knowles, says, "Great trainers [and mentors] love learning and are happiest when they are around its occurrence."[1] Such relationships are celebratory and affirming. As the mentor gives, the protégé reciprocates, and abundance begins to characterize the relationship. And there is never a possessive, credit-seeking dimension ("That's MY protégé").

Passion

Great mentoring partnerships are filled with passion; they are guided by mentors with deep feelings and a willingness to communicate those feelings. Passionate mentors recognize that effective learning has a vitality about it that is not logical, not rational, and not orderly. Such mentors get carried away with the spirit of the partnership and their feelings about the process of learning. Some may exude emotion quietly, but their cause-driven energy is clearly present. In a nutshell, mentors not only love the learning process, they love what the protégé can become—and they passionately demonstrate that devotion.

Courage

Mentoring takes courage; learning takes courage. Great mentors are allies of courage; they cultivate a partnership of courageousness. They take risks with learning, showing boldness in their efforts, and elicit courage in protégés by the examples they set. The preamble to learning is risk, the willingness to take a shaky step without the security of perfection. The preamble to risk is courage.

Ethics

Effective mentors must be clean in their learner-dealings, not false, manipulative, or greedy. Competent mentors must be honest and congruent in their communications and actions. They must not steal their learners' opportunities for struggle or moments of glory. Great mentors refrain from coveting their learners' talents or falsifying their own. They must honor the learner just as they honor the process of mutual learning.

Partnerships are the expectancy of the best in our abilities, attitudes, and aspirations. In a learning partnership, the mentor is not only helping the protégé but also continually communicating a belief that he or she is a fan of the learner. Partnerships are far more than good synergy. Great partnerships go beyond "greater than" to a realm of unforeseen worth. And worth in a mentoring partnership is laced with the equity of balance, the clarity of truth, the security of trust, the affirmation of abundance, the energy of passion, the boldness of courage, and the grounding of ethics.

The Real Aim of Mentoring: Mastering, Not Mastery

George is someone who has never been a person of moderation. When George was in college, he joined a group of fellow wayward students to take a forbidden midnight swim in the pool at the girls' gym on the other side of a tall, locked chain-link fence. George was the one who decided everyone should make it a skinny-dipping adventure. The fact that George was the only one who stripped never seemed to bother him. It was not surprising that years later, after reading the best-selling book *Swim with the Sharks without Being Eaten Alive*, George went to a pet store and boldly bought a live shark for his Miami apartment. Though less than a foot long, it was a real shark—with a distinctive white dorsal fin rising out of its gun-metal-gray body. George named the little fish Harvey after the book's author, Harvey Mackay.

Sometime later, George's life took an unexpected turn. He was promoted to regional sales manager of his company and transferred to Houston. Knowing he was going to be on the road a lot, George worried about who would take care of little Harvey. So he gave the shark to Sea World in Orlando. Harvey moved from a two-gallon fish bowl to an aquarium the size of a three-story house.

Several years went by. When George got married, the inextinguishable kid in George picked Walt Disney World as the perfect honeymoon site. While he and his wife were in Orlando, they decided to go by Sea World and check on little Harvey. They were stunned. Harvey now was almost ten feet long and weighed nearly five hundred pounds.

When George told one of us about Harvey, we thought it was another of his tall tales. But George was convincing. Apparently certain animals—like sharks, and like humans—grow commensurately with their surroundings. Google it if you don't believe us! If we are to grow to our greatest potential, we need a safe and unrestricted environment.

To grow is fundamentally the act of expanding, an unfolding into greatness. And so expansiveness is the most important attribute of a great mentoring relationship. Mentoring effectiveness is all about clearing an emotional path to make the learning journey as free of boundaries as possible. Change is a door opened from the inside. But it is the mentoring relationship that delivers the key to that door.

The real aim of mentoring is not mastery. Mastery implies closure, an ending, arrival at a destination. In today's ever-changing world, the goal is "mastering," a never-ending, ever-expansive journey of perpetual growth. It suggests the relationship is more important than the goal, that the process is more valued than the outcome.

Busting the Boundaries

So what can a mentor do to set up an expansive, boundary-free learning environment? Extensive research shows that great mentors give unswerving attention to four essential components: focus, feeling, family, and freedom.

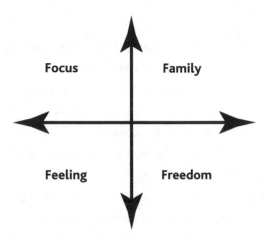

Figure 1. Components of Expansive Learning Environments

Focus

There are several ways adult learning (andragogy) is different from child learning (pedagogy). Adults are motivated to learn when they perceive an immediate or short-term rationale for that learning. You can tell a child, "This history you are learning in the classroom may not be useful on the playground at recess, but *someday* it will be helpful to you" and retain their interest. Adults are not so gullible. Granted, some adults get a kick out of learning purely for learning's sake, but they are in the minority. Most adults are motivated to learn if the effort will have a clear payoff in the present or—at most—in the very near future.

The mentoring partnership must be conducted so that the protégé knows the purpose of the learning. There needs to be an "as a result of this learning, you will be able to..." component woven through your partnership. In the organizational context, it helps to anchor the learning to the unit or organizational vision or mission, to unit objectives, and to the protégé's personal or professional goals and aspirations. The tie must be subtle... and at the same time obvious. It should be an initial focus... and a perpetual one. Anchoring learning to objectives is one way to create useful guideposts for measuring success. Think of focus as not only the basis for your interaction but as the very language you speak.

Feeling

Do you remember what you learned about relationships when you were in high school? Remember that friendship that went sour and how you worked so hard to get it back together? Remember going steady, breaking up, having fights, making up... and on and on? The lessons learned in those heart-pain days seem indelibly etched in our memories. They are the lessons we teach our children, nieces or nephews, or friends' children.

Now think about other things you learned in high school. Maybe you learned sine, cosine, and tangent. You learned to conjugate verbs and diagram sentences. You knew the length of the Amazon River, the height of the Empire State Building and could name the capital of every state in the union—including South Dakota and Kentucky! And you probably got A's on those tests. Remember? If there were a pop quiz today, how would you fare? Somehow, most learning that is not anchored to the heart is not retained.

The mentoring relationship is at its best when it is conducted with spirit and emotion. Talk with someone who has served in a combat role in war. They can tell you intricate details of the conflicts but only vaguely about the time spent in training. The lessons learned in combat were lessons of the heart, imprinted with the passion of the most exhilarating highs and the most depressing lows. Part of the mentor's job is to foster an environment where feelings, emotions, and learning are tightly linked.

Family

Mentoring works best when implemented in the spirit of partnership. In *The Fifth Discipline*, Peter Senge talks about another's "fellowship" as a key support for learning, but we think "family" is a better "f" word to capture the spirit of partnership. Fellowship could be simply an association, but "family" implies a much deeper relationship. Learning requires risk taking and experimentation. It necessitates error and mistake. It is uniquely difficult for a mentor to carry out an insight goal (fostering discovery) from an in-charge (I'm the boss) role. Even if the mentor is not in a functional managerial role, simply being an "expert" creates the potential of unequal power. Applied to mentor and protégé, "family" implies a close relationship, not a parent-child relationship. The goal is partnership.

Freedom

The ultimate test of the expansiveness of the mentoring relationship is when the learner is set free. Mentoring relationships are exercises in ceaseless letting go. Few conditions do a greater disservice to the protégé than mentor dependence. Dependence leads to protégé uncertainty and insecurity. Dependence results in a relationship that is inefficient and barren of worth to either mentor or protégé. Dependence implies the mentor is the sole repository of the wisdom required by the protégé.

Engendering freedom is all about creating strength and courage. Fostering freedom is also about building bridges to other resources, including linking the protégé up with other mentors. It means helping the protégé connect with a storehouse of resources to be accessed as needed.

SAGE: The Model for Great Mentoring

If the aim is to nurture "mastering"—through a mentoring partnership focused on learner discovery and independence, in a climate that reduces boundaries and encourages risk—what are the steps or stages needed to reach that aim?

The mentoring model found in this book is built around the belief that great mentoring requires four core competencies, each of which can be applied in many ways. These competencies form the sequential steps in the process of mentoring. All four have been selected for their ability to blend effectively. Not accidentally, the first letters of these four competencies (and steps) spell the word "SAGE"—a helpful mnemonic as well as a symbolic representation of the goal, the power-free facilitation of learning. They are:

Surrendering—leveling the learning field;

Accepting—creating a safe haven for risk taking;

Gifting—the core contributions of the mentor, the Main Event; and

Extending—nurturing protégé independence.

Surrendering

Most leaders are socially conditioned to *drive* the process of learning; great mentors *surrender* to it. Driving the process has many unfortunate effects. It tends to cause resistance; it minimizes the potential for serendipitous growth, and it tilts the focus from competence to control.

If there is one word many leaders hate, it is the word "surrender." However, by "surrender" we don't mean losing but yielding to a flow greater than either player in the process. The dictionary defines "surrender" as "to yield possession of." Mentors who attempt to hold, own, or control the process deprive their protégés of the freedom needed to foster discovery.

Surrendering is the process of leveling the learning field. Most mentoring relationships begin with mentor and protégé in unequal power positions . . . boss to subordinate, master to novice, or teacher to student. The risk is that power creates anxiety and anxiety minimizes risk taking—that ever-important ingredient required for growth. Surrendering encompasses all the actions the mentor takes to pull power and authority out of the mentoring relationship so protégé anxiety is lowered and courage is heightened.

Accepting

Accepting is the act of inclusion. Acceptance is what renowned psychologist Carl Rogers labeled "unconditional positive regard." Most managers are taught to focus on exclusion. Exclusion is associated with preferential treatment, presumption, arrogance, and insolence—growth killers all. The verb "accept," however, implies ridding oneself of bias, preconceived judgments, and human labeling. Accepting is embracing, rather than evaluating or judging.

Accepting is code for creating an egalitarian, safe haven for learning. When mentors demonstrate noticeable curiosity, they telegraph acceptance. When mentors encourage and support, they send a message that safety abounds. Protégés need safety in the mentoring relationship in order to undertake experimental behavior in the face of public vulnerability.

Gifting

Gifting is the act of generosity. Gifting, as opposed to giving, means bestowing something of value upon another without expecting anything in return. Mentors have many gifts to share. When they bestow those gifts abundantly and unconditionally, they strengthen the relationship and keep it healthy. Gifting is the antithesis of taking or using manipulatively. It is at the opposite end of the spectrum from greed.

Gifting is often seen as the main event of mentoring. Mentors *gift* advice, they *gift* feedback, they *gift* focus and direction, they *gift* the proper balance between intervening and letting protégés test their wings, and they *gift* their passion for learning. However, just as we all recoil at the sound of "Let me give you some advice," protégés must be ready for the mentor's gifts. Surrendering and accepting are important initial steps in creating a readiness in the protégé. Gifts are wasted when they are not valued—when they are discounted and discarded.

Extending

Extending means pushing the relationship beyond its expected boundaries. Mentors who extend are those willing to give up the relationship in the interest of growth, to seek alternative ways to foster growth. They recognize that the protégé's learning can occur and be enhanced in many and mysterious ways. Extending is needed to create an independent self-directed learner.

Surrendering, accepting, gifting, and extending are the capabilities or proficiencies required for the mentor to be an effective partner in the protégé's growth. These four core competencies also serve as the organizing structure for the rest of this book. Their sequence is important. The process of mentoring begins with surrendering and ends with extending. Under each of the four competencies you will find several chapters full of techniques for demonstrating that competence effectively.

Mentoring is an honor. Except for love, there is no greater gift one can give another than the gift of growth. It is a rare privilege to help another learn, have the relevant wisdom to be useful to another, and partner with someone who can benefit from that wisdom. This book is crafted with a single goal: to help you exercise that honor and privilege in a manner that benefits you and all those you influence.

2

Mentoring in Action
The Act of Mentoring Up Close

A successful career will no longer be about promotion. It will be about mastery.

Michael Hammer, author of *Reengineering the Corporation*

Jack Gamble was the consummate outdoorsman. Every deer, dove, quail, turkey, and largemouth bass was in grave danger whenever Jack entered the wild with his rifle, shotgun, bow, or reel. But at Gracie-Omar, Inc., he was the consummate mentor.

Jack was the manufacturing engineering manager at the Triplin, Georgia, plant of Gracie-Omar, a large computer-systems and components plant. He had done his time in the trenches and had quickly worked his way up the chain. Now he reported directly to the plant manager. Jack's upward mobility was due not only to his superior performance and down-home humor but to his unique way of communicating to associates what he learned. As the plant expanded, the plant manager promoted Jack repeatedly, seeing him as the prototype of a "learning organization leader."

Tracy Black was a new systems engineer transferred to Gracie-Omar's Triplin plant from their plant north of Boston. Tracy would ultimately be assigned to Jack and had nothing in common with him except hunting. Tracy was from upstate New York; Jack was local, born and raised twenty-five miles from Triplin. Tracy had a somber and clipped style; Jack had a mile-wide smile and a drawl as slow as molasses. Tracy was a liberal Democrat and Catholic; Jack was a deacon in the Baptist church and a conservative Republican. Not least, Tracy was a woman; Jack was not.

Tracy and Jack first met at the company picnic. It was Tracy's second day. She arrived thirty minutes late. The only people she knew were the human resources director who had interviewed her, and Rod, the plant manager, whom she had briefly met. The crowd seemed very cliquish to her, their boisterous conversation like code: "We're all big buddies here, and if you're not one of us now, you won't be in this lifetime!" The meeting planner announced how the meal would be served, the plant manager made a short speech, and Jack told a long joke about a mule. The crowd laughed and cheered; she didn't understand what was funny about the punch line. She thought of Boston.

"Howdy," said someone behind her as she was reaching for a short ear of corn in a long serving line. Startled, she quickly turned. "I'm Jack Gamble. Rod tells me you and I will be working together."

Oh, no! she thought privately, Not the mule man! But she managed to utter a crisp hello.

Jack asked her the usual fair-weather, cocktail-party questions—where're you from, where'd you go to school, what'd you do before you came here, you want to sit? At the end of five minutes, Jack suggested that Tracy stop by his office on Monday right after lunch.

Jack's office revealed few clues about its occupant. As Tracy waited there for him to return from a luncheon meeting, she searched for clues about this man who would be her boss and mentor. On the desk was a picture of Jack's wife and two children; on the wall, a framed ISO-9001 certificate and a picture of two wild turkeys. On the floor behind the desk was a piece of equipment that looked like a large blue jug. Other than that, the office could have belonged to anyone.

"Sorry I'm late!" she heard from behind her. "Would you like a glass of real good homemade iced tea?" he asked with the same impish style he had used to tell the mule joke.

"No," said Tracy, more brusquely than she had intended.

Jack served himself from the large blue jug. He turned around as he began speaking, warmth and confidence in his words. "Tracy, I'm real excited about getting to work with you. Sarah, over in human resources, tells me you are one terrific systems engineer." Tracy didn't know how to respond, but Jack continued, not seeming to want a response from her yet. "You've worked on the LWB-211, which I would really like to know more about. We haven't gotten any of those in here yet, but we plan to in the fourth quarter.

"Now, how can I help you get settled in?" Tracy was not sure, but she asked Jack whether she would have access to the company cloud and a laptop with a superfast modem that would enable her to link into company files when she worked on the road.

"That's a new one," said Jack, writing it on a small pad. "I'll find out and let you know right away. I've been keeping a list of the questions new people ask, along with the answers. I've made you a copy. But the cloud question won't be in this issue!" Tracy was beginning to feel more comfortable with Jack.

"I don't know what you think of this plant," Jack went on, "but I sure do remember what I felt at first. It seemed like a tight family that didn't want any more cousins! I remember feeling downright scared and wondering if I'd made a bum decision. But I made up my mind I wasn't going to let it beat me. I just started acting like I was already in the family. And you know what? It worked like a thirty-ought-six on an eight-pointer at twenty yards!"

Tracy was surprised. "You're a hunter?" she asked.

Jack's eyes twinkled mischievously. He looked like someone who had been caught with his hand in the cookie jar. "You bet!"

he said. "And if you aren't, then I just messed in my nest—using an expression that only another hunter would get."

"I hunt too," replied Tracy, somewhat relieved to have one thing in common.

"Terrific!" said Jack. "Do you like to hunt deer?"

Tracy nodded. "I hunt anything in season," she said. It was her first foray into Southern mores.

Jack leaned forward. "That's great! Have you seen the new issue of *Field and Stream*?" She had not. "Well, I have it right here. Why don't you take it? There's a great article on deer stands—has some crazy ideas I plan to try next time my son and I go deer hunting." Tracy began to loosen up as they continued to talk for some time on their newfound common interest.

A few weeks after Jack and Tracy's get-acquainted meeting, an Ulmer-1911 machine was delivered. Jack had been Ulmer-qualified for a few years and had gone back to Wisconsin twice for refresher training. Tracy had heard about but never operated the machine and was eager to learn. Late one afternoon Jack and Tracy sat down for the first time at the console of the 1911.

"Before we start," Jack began, "I want to find out what you know about this machine." He listened as Tracy described the machine's purpose and what it could produce. "I see you've done your homework," he said proudly. Tracy smiled.

Jack continued: "Think of this machine as an extension of your right arm and imagine what it would feel like to have that arm ten feet longer than the other. Not only does hand-eye coordination change, but you're bound to feel awkward. Expect that same sensation with the Ulmer-1911."

Tracy began to feel a bit less apprehensive. "Are you going to show me how it works?" she asked, her impatience beginning to be evident.

"I was just like you," Jack teased, "as anxious as a long-tailed cat in a room full of rocking chairs." Tracy grinned and took a deep breath. "But," Jack continued, "it will be better for you to run this machine than to watch me run it. Just looking at the center screen, what do you think is the first step?"

Tracy quickly responded, "I'd say keying on command six and moving the dugen switch to ninety degrees."

"Great choice!" Jack answered. "And what's your objective in taking that route?"

The lesson continued until Tracy was operating the Ulmer fairly proficiently. The only time Jack touched the equipment was after Tracy had taken a series of incorrect steps and gotten so far off the starting point that she needed help getting back. Jack's goal was to guide her thinking and understanding more than her operating and remembering.

In the months that followed, Jack and Tracy's relationship improved. Their mutual interest in hunting turned out to be a key source of compatibility. As Tracy grew less nervous and more confident, she began to take more risks in her spirited interaction with Jack. Soon she was matching him jab for friendly jab. She also began assuming greater plant responsibility, including the supervision of four engineers.

One day she stopped Jack in the hall with a look of concern on her face. "Got a few minutes?" she asked.

Five minutes later they were in her office. "Adam's a problem," she began bluntly after Jack closed the door behind him.

She had learned that with Jack there was no need to beat around the bush. "Just cut to the chase," he had encouraged her. It had proven helpful in her dealings with some of the more impatient engineers.

"Tell me more," Jack replied, sitting in the chair in front of her desk.

Adam was one of Tracy's new direct reports. "He's not pulling his weight. I've encouraged him, counseled him, and tried to understand him. I'm running out of patience."

Jack waited to make sure she had no more to say about the subject. "How can I help?" he asked, not wanting to assume anything
yet about whether his assistance was required.

Tracy looked straight at him. "I guess I need you to be a sounding board, and maybe give me some ideas on how to get him fired
up—or fired."

"What do you think the problem is, based on what you know?"
asked Jack.

"His morale is lousy. When I try to talk with him about his performance, his nonverbals are rather patronizing, like he's offended
that I raised the issue."

Jack thought for a minute. "I can see that would be a tough nut
to crack. I've never been really comfortable dealing with negative
performers. It always makes me feel anxious if I have to get tough
with an employee. I can see—"

"But you still manage to get them turned around," interrupted
Tracy.

Jack could see that Tracy thought he had some magical secret
he had kept to himself. "You believe there's a special technique that
maybe you've missed."

"Yes, I suppose I do, in a way. You make it look easy. I remember when you had to terminate Edsel Joiner. The guy ended
up thanking you for it!"

Jack did not respond for a while. Tracy suddenly felt awkward,
as though she had allowed her stream of emotion to overflow its
banks. Then, with unusual emotion in his voice, Jack said, "That
was the scariest thing I've ever done since I came to work here."
They both sat in silence.

Jack took another stab at the issue. "How does he react when
you get stern and serious?"

"I'm not sure," Tracy responded.

Jack tried again. "Let me ask it this way: if I asked Adam to
candidly describe you when the two of you talk about his performance, what words would he use?"

Tracy's demeanor began to change. It was as if the wheels of wisdom were turning in her head.

"He would say I was relentlessly patient." She was still half lost in thought.

"What else?"

Tracy responded with near excitement in her voice. "He would *not* describe me as tough, demanding, or disciplined."

Jack sensed that she was solving her own issue. Again, he paused before raising another question. He knew instinctively that pace was everything when insight was the goal. "So what do you think should be your next step?"

Tracy began to outline steps: a serious conversation, a performance plan, short-term goals with clear feedback, supervision with a shorter leash, and, above all, less understanding and more discipline. Jack offered a few ideas, but mostly affirmation and encouragement. They parted with an agreement to revisit the issue in a few days.

The story had a happy ending. Adam admitted to Tracy that he was having difficulty working for a woman, but he ultimately grew to respect her, turning out excellent performance. Tracy was promoted to department manager and then transferred to corporate headquarters in Wisconsin. Jack mentored more new engineers. He was offered promotions but turned down any that involved a move. Woods for hunting were more important than mahogany row. Besides, he got a kick out of watching people learn—especially those who weren't sure they were going to fit in.

3

Assessing Your Mentoring Talents

A Self-Check Scale

He who knows others is learned; he who knows himself is wise.

Lao-tzu, *Tao Te Ching*

Self-assessment: does the term make you think of navel gazing? Perhaps you've had enough of the joys of testing, performance reviews, exams, and the like. For many, testing feels more about masochism than mastery! However, drawing a finer bead on our gifts and blind spots is a precursor to improvement and growth—and that, after all, is what mentoring is all about.

The Mentor Scale is a painless way to determine what personal attributes you bring to the mentoring relationship. The goal is not to judge, evaluate, or criticize you as a person; there are no right or wrong answers. The objective is to offer you a picture of your gifts and your potential blind spots. For example, if a person knows he or she has a tendency to procrastinate, that person can take steps to counter that tendency, to break the habit of putting things off until the last minute.

At this point, you may be thinking of zipping past this chapter.

Please resist the temptation. We encourage you to work through the self-assessment. There will be many references to it throughout the rest of the book. If you haven't done it, you will miss out on some potentially powerful mentoring insights. You do not have to put your answers in the book; simply write them on a separate sheet of paper. This way you can easily review your answers as we revisit the Mentor Scale at various points throughout the book.

Now, pencil ready? Here goes . . .

The "Test"

The Mentor Scale on the following pages lists thirty-nine sentence stems, each with two possible endings. Keeping your work environment in mind, quickly review each item and circle the letter of the ending that best completes the sentence. Read each item carefully, but choose your response quickly. Instruments like this tend to be more accurate if you go with your immediate reaction rather than pondering your choice. Do not leave items blank. You will find some items in which neither choice is perfectly accurate. Select the one that seems better. After completing the inventory, proceed to the scoring form.

The Mentor Scale

1. People probably see me as
   a. hard-nosed   b. a soft touch
2. Work days I like the most are
   a. unpredictable   b. planned
3. When it comes to celebrations, most organizations need
   a. fewer   b. more
4. When I evaluate people, my decisions are based on
   a. justice   b. mercy
5. My approach to planning my personal activities is
   a. easygoing   b. orderly

6. People generally see me as a person who is

                a. formal   b. personable

7. When it comes to social situations, I tend to

                a. hold back   b. jump in

8. I like to spend my leisure time in ways that are fairly

                a. spontaneous   b. routine

9. I believe leaders should be more concerned about employee

                a. rights   b. feelings

10. When I encounter people in need of help, I'm more likely to

                a. avoid   b. pitch in

11. When I am in a group, I typically

                a. follow   b. lead

12. Most people see me as

                a. private   b. open

13. My friends know that I am

                a. firm   b. gentle

14. If I were in a group of strangers, people would most likely remember me as a

                a. listener   b. leader

15. When it comes to expressing my feelings, most people probably see me as

                a. guarded   b. comfortable

16. When people I depend on make mistakes, I am typically

                a. patient   b. impatient

17. When I eat out, I generally order food that

                a. sounds unique b. I know I like

18. In general, I prefer

                a. the theater   b. a party

19. In a conflict, when anger is involved, my emotional fuse is usually

                a. short   b. long

20. In an emergency situation, I would likely be
                    a. calm   b. anxious
21. I prefer to express myself to others in ways that are
                    a. indirect   b. direct
22. I am likely to be ruled by
                    a. logic   b. emotion
23. When in new and unfamiliar situations, I am usually
                    a. carefree   b. careful
24. In a festive social situation, I am usually
                    a. passive   b. active
25. When I am blamed for something I did not cause,
    my initial reaction is to
                    a. listen   b. defend
26. If I am in a situation in which I lose
    or am left disappointed, I get
                    a. sad   b. mad
27. If someone came to me in tears,
    I would probably feel
                    a. awkward   b. at home
28. Most people see me as
                    a. an optimist   b. a pessimist
29. People usually see me as
                    a. uncritical   b. critical
30. If people were given a forced choice, they would say I was
                    a. too quiet   b. too loud
31. At the end of a long party, I usually find myself
                    a. exhausted   b. energized
32. When I work on projects, I am best at getting them
                    a. started   b. completed
33. I believe people should approach their work with
                    a. dedication   b. inspiration
34. My social blunders typically leave me
                    a. embarrassed   b. amused

35. When my organization announces
    a major change, I get
                              a. excited   b. concerned
36. People are likely to see me as
                              a. firm   b. warm
37. After a tough day, I like to unwind
                              a. alone   b. with others
38. Change is most often your
                              a. friend   b. adversary
39. My work and social life
                              a. are separate   b. often overlap

The Scoring Form

Sociability

Using simple hatch marks, tally your A's and B's for the thirteen sociability items.

    1, 4, 7, 10, 13, 16, 19, 22, 25, 28, 31, 34, 37

	A	B
Totals	_____	_____

Dominance

Do the same for the thirteen dominance items...

    2, 5, 8, 11, 14, 17, 20, 23, 26, 29, 32, 35, 38

	A	B
Totals	_____	_____

Openness

...and for the thirteen openness items.

    3, 6, 9, 12, 15, 18, 21, 24, 27, 30, 33, 36, 39

	A	B
Totals	_____	_____

Interpretation

The Mentor Scale is inspired by the FIRO-B®, an excellent instrument developed by Will Schutz and distributed exclusively by Consulting Psychologists Press, Mountain View, California (www.cpp.com).[1] The scale measures—at one point in time—a mentor's need for sociability, dominance, and openness, all crucial components of an effective mentoring relationship. (Schutz's FIRO-B® instrument labels these components "inclusion," "control," and "affection," respectively.)

Sociability has to do with your preference for being with or apart from others. People with high column A scores in sociability tend to be reserved loners; those with high column B scores tend to be outgoing joiners. People with similar numbers of A's and B's are neither highly sociable nor highly reserved; they can be moderately sociable or moderately reserved, depending on the situation.

What does sociability have to do with mentoring? People who have high sociability scores will find the rapport-building and dialogue-leading dimensions of mentoring easier. They will have to work hard to avoid dominating discussions. Low sociability scores are found among people whose reserve may make them a bit unapproachable. These people will need to work harder at helping protégés open up and communicate.

Dominance is about your preference regarding being in charge. People with high column A scores are comfortable having someone else do the leading and often prefer it. People with high column B scores tend to like being in control and often assert that need. Low dominance scores can also indicate a high need for independence. People with balanced scores are neither highly dominant nor highly submissive. They can control moderately or not at all, depending on the situation.

Dominance is a major issue in mentoring with a partnering philosophy. The whole concept of mentoring today is based on a relationship of shared power. High dominance scorers are reluctant either to give up control or to share control of the relationship; they have to work hard to listen rather than talk. Low dominance scorers, on the other hand, may need to work to assume leadership of the relationship. They may take such a low-key, laissez-faire approach that the protégé feels insecure and without guidance.

Openness refers to how easily you trust others. High column A scores are found among people who are cautious, guarded, and reluctant to show feelings. High column B scores are typical of people with many close relationships, who are comfortable being vulnerable and tend to express their feelings easily. People with similar A and B scores are moderately open or moderately cautious, depending on the situation.

High openness scorers will find it easy to reveal themselves in a mentoring relationship. In fact, their challenge is to be candid and open enough to encourage the protégé to do likewise, while not being so aggressive as to overwhelm or intimidate the protégé. Low openness scorers, however, will need to work at overcoming their caution in order to take early emotional and interpersonal risks with the protégé; their instinctive guardedness can make the protégé feel that mistakes might have dire consequences.

Several chapters ahead have sidebars addressing the implications of your Mentor Scale scores in terms of each chapter's issues and challenges. The goal is to show you how to use your strengths and compensate for your weaknesses. Is it possible to be too sociable or too open? Of course! Is it not important in some situations to be highly dominant? Again, of course! For effective mentoring, however, our view is that you push toward the high side of sociability and openness, toward the low side of dominance.

Remember, the Mentor Scale gives you a reading at a moment in time, one that may change with the circumstances. Keep in mind also that the scale assesses only three aspects of your leadership personality. Don't generalize the results beyond their intent; too often, personality instruments are used to label or categorize people, to discount their individual uniqueness. Learn from the Mentor Scale—but avoid using the results as though they were holy writ.

4

Every Knock's a Boost

An Interview with Mark Tercek, President
and CEO of The Nature Conservancy

How would you describe your most important mentor?

My most important mentor is a guy I worked with for years. He was my boss and then became a peer. He always told me in a very direct way what he thought I should do in difficult circumstances. In my heart of hearts, I already knew his advice was the right thing to do. But I would try to rationalize not doing it because it was the awkward stuff. He was a good mentor because he would make me do it. "You have to do X, Y, and Z," he would say, and there was no alternative. Even if it was difficult, it was always the right thing to do to move things forward. He never offered me the easy way out.

What traits were most instrumental in his work with you?

His willingness to give me advice I'd rather not hear. He was insistent and he overcame my objections. He was kind of annoying, to be honest, but he didn't care. He put giving me good advice over being liked. And he gave his advice in an irritating, lecturing way. But it was good advice, so I kept going back for more.

When he was no longer my boss, I'd still go to him for advice. But at some point in my career, I remember thinking very clearly, I don't really need his advice anymore. I now know to do the things he advises me to do. Now he is more of a friend than a mentor. He liked being a mentor, and the more people he mentored, the better he got at it.

What is one example or incident or illustration of how this person was helpful to you?

Years ago, I was working an investment banking transaction in Asia. It was a public offering of stock, and the deal was going very badly by the standards of that day. Today it might not have been a big deal, but it was back then. I was a mid-level person at the organization, and the people who ran the firm were very concerned.

In the middle of the night (in Asia), I talked with my mentor. He told me I needed to call the number two person at the firm and tell him what was going on. It was scary. This person was intimidating and it was his part of the firm that represented the clients who had bought the stock that was now going down. He was likely going to be angry and unsympathetic. I didn't want to call him.

My mentor said, "You have to call him. One, he needs to hear these things directly from you. He needs to hear your side of the story. Two, you are doing all the right things to deal with this tough circumstance. This is an opportunity for you to show him that, even if he is unfriendly or critical or it feels like a bad conversation. You'll be showing him you are not afraid, that you are going to do the right thing, and that he and the firm should have confidence in you."

My mentor often told me, "Every knock's a boost." I was in a tough situation, but the fact that people would try to blame it on me was actually a boost. Why? Because all eyes were on me. It was an opportunity to show people what I could do. And I did. Sure, it was awkward and unpleasant, but I did the right things, given the circumstances, and the senior executive was probably favorably impressed.

Without my mentor's insistence that I deal with the issue directly, the senior executive would have seen only the negative. He would have thought we weren't doing what was right to deal with the circumstance. It wasn't easy, but it was the right thing to do. I knew this in my gut, but my mentor gave me the push I needed. He didn't recommend I do it, or suggest that I might consider it. Instead, he said, "Call him now. Every knock is a boost. You'll be fine. Do it now!" It did become a high-profile challenge, and people got to watch me in action because I was the person on the scene. I dealt with it well. If I had ducked the knock, someone else would have gotten the boost.

What other advice or feedback did he give you?

He advised me to take charge in difficult situations, to step up and take responsibility even when circumstances were tough. When you're leading a firm through tough situations in a responsible and smart way, there's no time for placing blame or being defensive. He also helped me handle interpersonal issues. If I was dealing with a tough personality, he'd say, "Go see the person right now. Don't leave them a voice mail. Don't send them an e-mail. Go look them in the eye and tell them what you are doing. Don't make it complicated; just get in front of it."

He gave me another kind of advice when I was in a new job. He told me to meet with as many people as I could and ask them for any input, guidance, feedback, and suggestions they might have. And then shut up and listen.

Whether advising me on difficult situations or on starting a new job, there was a running theme to all of his advice: the best path is usually the most direct one. Get in front of people and address head-on whatever might need to be addressed.

I'm enormously grateful to my mentor, and when I've had the opportunity, I've tried to be a good mentor just like he was.

SURRENDERING— LEVELING THE LEARNING FIELD

If the impulse to daring and bravery is too fierce and violent, stay it with guidance and instruction.

Xun Zi

"Siamese twins!" whispered the silver-headed, elegantly dressed woman to her friend seated beside her. "They dance like two people who are one." Her colleague nodded with enthusiastic agreement as they watched the two dancers merge, spin, disengage, reemerge in a human blend as harmonious as light with shadow. "They are magic in motion," the friend whispered back.

Mentoring at its best is a partnership, like two dancers perfectly in sync. Partnership learning positions both parties—mentor and protégé—on a collective journey of discovery. As the mentor embraces a curious, egalitarian stance, the protégé instinctively senses safety and joins in the journey. The more the mentor seeks to learn (rather than just teach), the more the protégé feels affirmed and less alone. Mentoring is a dance of sorts to reach the heights of a pure partnership. And it all begins with surrendering to the process of learning instead of pursuing the program of teaching. We will first explore the essence of partnership as the preferred path for mentoring.

Partnerships are journeys in becoming. They are always divine relationships in the making. They are hopeful pursuits of magic, not efforts valued only at completion. Some otherwise successful partnerships are susceptible to what we will label the "perfection trap." And focus on flawlessness is a dead-end duality path. The by-product of this right-wrong/good-bad thinking is the seed of win-lose paradigms which fuel competitive relationships.

Partnerships impeccably performed look like "magic in motion." The relationship is a living demonstration of wild-river efficiency mixed with barnyard harmony. To spectators on the outside, the flow seems magical. To the participants in the midst of the collaborative current that same flow feels like a spiritual surprise.

The workings of partnerships, however, are far from magical. Like magicians, partnerships present an orchestrated demonstration of proficiencies and disposition. Both skill and attitude must work in harmony for a winning performance. A technically accurate magician with no showmanship or flair would be no more successful as a true magician than a bumbling sleight-of-hand act with personality plus.

How does this high-octane learning occur? What action does the mentor need to take to encourage this synergistic moment with a protégé? In a word, *surrender*. The magical first step is to surrender to the process.

Surrendering means completely relinquishing any effort to control or manipulate the outcome. Surrendering means putting all effort into being completely authentic, real, and mask-free. Surrendering means being devoted to learning, not dedicated to convincing. As management consultant Bruce Fritch says, "Surrendering is the most difficult and most courageous interpersonal act a leader can take with a subordinate. It is also the most powerful!"

Mentors surrender in several ways. One of these could be called "mask removal"—the willingness to be open and vulnerable. We all wear masks, in part to protect ourselves against rejection. When a mentor removes this mask in front of the protégé, it changes the nature of the relationship from cautious to unguarded. Energy normally devoted to cover and protection becomes available for insight and discovery.

An associate of ours, a gifted consulting psychologist, taught a series of executive workshops on performance coaching. The final advice he gave attendees was to practice their newfound skills on a couple of subordinates within the coming week: "Start your practice by telling your associates something like the following: 'I have just attended a workshop on performance coaching and learned some new skills I want to use in our relationship. I will be very awkward at first and make a lot of mistakes, but with some practice and your patience, I will get better. And we will both benefit.'"

The advice was a valuable relationship builder. Attendees at follow-up sessions reported enormous success. The authenticity caused subordinates to see their leaders in a new light. Many reported that their sessions with subordinates turned out to be the single most powerful and productive conversation they had ever had. The typical executive report went something like this: "When I gave up trying to force it to work, it seemed to take on a life of its own and steered the relationship where it needed to go. It was amazing. I have never felt anything like it. It was like magic." This like-magic quality of mentoring begins to happen with surrendering.

Surrendering is fundamentally about being assertively honest and candid, with the intention of helping, not hurting, the other person. There is a cleanness and frankness about relationships in which authenticity is valued. Great mentors care enough to be honest and forthright; they are also curious and learning-oriented enough to invite and accept candor from the protégé.

5

Kindling Kinship
The Power of Rapport

Real education consists of drawing the best out of yourself.

Mohandas Gandhi

"Rapport" comes from an old French word that means "a bringing back" or "harmony renewed." This definition reminds us that rapport is fundamentally about actions aimed at restoring the security of the bond with which we begin life. Life, for most of us, does not start with anxiety or fear. Life begins with security and trust. The path from dependence to independence teaches us about rejection, discomfort, and pain. We protect ourselves with the shield of personality (the Greek word for "personality" means "mask") and assume that each new relationship is a threat until shown otherwise. The ritual of relationship is the gradual lowering of the mask.

The success of a mentoring relationship can hang on the first encounters between mentor and protégé. The tone set in that first meeting can determine whether the relationship will be fruitful or fraught with fear and anxiety. Rapport building expedites shield lowering; quality learning will not occur until the shield has been lowered enough for the learner to take risks in front of the mentor. As the person who is usually in the driver's seat at the outset of the relationship, the mentor must ensure a good start—the renewal of the original bond.

Can a mentoring relationship get back on track if the first encounter falters? Of course—and thank goodness. Most of us can remember a solid friendship that started out on shaky ground. We also remember how long it took and how much energy had to be expended to overcome that rocky beginning. But the sooner we can establish rapport, the more time and energy we save—and the sooner the relationship moves onto solid ground, the faster learning can occur. Telling a funny story to open a speech, making small talk to kick off a sales call, and the old Southern custom of bringing a gift when visiting a friend, all acknowledge that openings are potentially rocky *and* important.

The Components of Rapport

What does rapport building entail for a mentor? How does the mentor establish early kinship, trust, and comfort? What follows is a discussion of the four components of rapport: leveling communications, gifting gestures, receptivity for feelings, and reflective responses. (Okay, there are probably twenty-five components—or twenty-five hundred—but in this book we will work with four. We all know there is not a finite number of most things, especially in areas like habits, wonders of the world, ways to leave your lover, or components of rapport. The four here were chosen for convenience and workability.) The point is, develop your own techniques for rapport building, consistent with the spirit of these components. To jump-start your efforts, we've included several applications in each section.

Leveling Communications

Rapport begins with the sights and sounds of openness and positive regard. Any normal person approaching a potentially anxious encounter will raise his antennae high in search of clues about the road ahead: Will this situation embarrass me? Will this person take advantage of me? Will I be effective in this encounter? Is there harm awaiting me?

Given the protégé's search for early warning signs, the mentor must be quick to transmit signals of welcome. An open posture (for example, no crossed arms), warm and enthusiastic gestures, eye contact, removing physical barriers, and personalized greetings all communicate a desire for a level playing field. Mentors who broadcast power signals (peering over an imposing desk, making the protégé do all the approaching, tight and closed body language, a reserved manner, or facial expressions that telegraph distance) risk complete failure to establish a good mentoring partnership.

Gifting Gestures

The opening communication can signal only that the path ahead may be safe for travel; it does not ensure rapport. The "Actions speak louder than words" adage is uniquely fitting at this juncture. Protégés need a gesture or action that they can take as a token of affinity.

Establishing rapport is a bit like courtship. You don't say, "Hi, I'm Bill. Let's get married. How's tomorrow at three?" There are the little matters of dating, gifts, parties, meeting the family, showers, ministers—all the preliminaries needed for a long-lasting and rewarding relationship.

The best mentors are especially creative with these signals. The perfunctory "How about a cup of coffee?" is certainly a well-worn gifting gesture. However, think about how much more powerful a statement like "I had my assistant locate this article I thought you might find useful" could be as early evidence that the relationship will be a friendly one. One effective mentor kept a supply of his wife's homemade jellies for visitors. The gift was always bestowed early in the encounter, not at the end.

There are as many ways to signal benign intent as there are mentors and protégés. Find one that suits you and works for your associates.

Receptivity for Feelings

The great psychologist Carl Rogers wrote extensively on unconditional positive regard and its impact on relationships. His research repeatedly affirmed the role such a generous attitude has on psychological healing and wellness. A good mentor establishes rapport through careful attentiveness to the protégé's feelings early in the encounter. When people believe they are heard and understood, they feel secure and comfortable. Establishing rapport is not about asking, "How are you feeling?" It is about listening intently to ascertain the feelings behind the words—and making responses that acknowledge these feelings.

In her article "What Exactly Is Charisma?" Patricia Sellers profiles Orit Gadiesh, the former chair of the prestigious global management consulting firm Bain & Company: "Orit has that talent for making you feel you're the most important person in the room. She bleeds your blood." One way she makes clients feel important, reports Sellers, is by never looking at her watch. Inside Bain, Gadiesh was regarded as a junior consultant's most generous mentor.[1]

In her story "Mockingbirds," Mary Oliver tells of an elderly couple visited by strangers in their poor abode. Lacking any goods to offer their visitors, the couple simply listens to their guests with all their heart. The strangers turn out to be gods who view the couple's attentiveness as the very best gift humans can give.[2] Gods and protégés are moved and mellowed by mentors who listen from the heart. As a mentor, continually ask yourself: "What must he or she be feeling right now? How might I feel if our roles were reversed?"

Reflective Responses

Receptivity to the protégé's feelings enables you to provide a tailor-made reflective response that says, "I've been there as well." This gesture, another way of saying, "I am similar to you," promotes the kinship and closeness that are vital to trust. The goal is empathetic identification. Empathy is different from sympathy. The word "sympathy" comes from the Greek word *sympatheia*, meaning "shared feeling." Empathy means "in-feeling," or the ability to understand another's feelings. Relationship strength is not spawned by "Misery loves company"; it comes through "I've been there too" identification.

Reflective responses can be as simple as a short personal story that lets the protégé know that you appreciate his feelings. Mildly self-deprecating anecdotes can work well, too. Above all, rapport is best served by humility and sensitivity. If you feel awkward, say you do. If you feel excited, say so. The sooner you speak your feelings, the faster the protégé will match your vulnerability.

These ideas about rapport are meant to spark your thinking seriously about how to begin this important getting-started phase of mentoring. However, you should also keep in mind that the main ingredient in the recipe for rapport is authenticity. The more you surrender to who you are in front of the protégé, the more at home she will feel. Compatibility is as vital in mentoring as in any other important relationship. How quickly and effectively that compatibility is established can make a major difference in how competent the protégé becomes.

Jack Gamble on Rapport

("Mentoring In Action" Revisited)

"Sorry I'm late!" she heard from behind her. "Would you like a glass of real good homemade iced tea?" he asked with the same impish style he had used to tell the mule joke.

"No," said Tracy, more brusquely than she had intended.

Jack served himself from the large blue jug. He turned as he began speaking, warmth and confidence in his words. "Tracy, I'm real excited about getting to work with you. Sarah, over in human resources, tells me you are one terrific systems engineer." Tracy didn't know how to respond, but Jack continued, not seeming to want a response from her yet. "You've worked on the LWB-211, which I would really like to know more about. We haven't gotten any of those in here yet, but we plan to in the fourth quarter.

"Now, how can I help you get settled in?" Tracy was not sure, but she asked Jack whether she would be getting a laptop with a high speed modem that would enable her to link into the company intranet when she worked on the road.

"That's a new one," said Jack, writing it on a small pad. "I'll find out and let you know right away. I've been keeping a list of the questions new people ask, along with the answers. I've made you a copy. But the modem question won't be in this issue!" Tracy was beginning to feel more comfortable with Jack.

"I don't know what you think of this plant," Jack went on, "but I sure do remember what I felt at first. It seemed like a tight family that didn't want any more cousins! I remember feeling downright scared and wondering if I'd made a bum decision. But I made up my mind I wasn't going to let it beat me. I just started acting like I was already in the family. And you know what? It worked like a thirty-ought-six on an eight-pointer at twenty yards!"

Tracy was surprised. "You're a hunter?" she asked.

Jack's eyes twinkled mischievously. He looked like someone who had been caught with his hand in the cookie jar. "You bet!" he said. "And if you aren't, then I just messed in my nest—using an expression that only another hunter would get."

"I hunt too," replied Tracy, somewhat relieved to have one thing in common.

"Terrific!" said Jack. "Do you like to hunt deer?"

Tracy nodded. "I hunt anything in season," she said. It was her first foray into Southern mores.

Jack leaned forward. "That's great! Have you seen the new issue of *Field and Stream?*" She had not. "Well, I have it right here. Why don't you take it? There's a great article on deer stands—has some crazy ideas I plan to try next time my son and I go deer hunting." Tracy began to loosen up as they continued to talk for some time on their newfound common interest.

6

The Elements of Trust Making
"This Could Be the Start of Something Big!"

Most of the advice we receive from others is not so much evidence of their affection for us, as it is evidence of their affection for themselves.

Josh Billings

"I'll be back to get you when school is out," a parent promises as her youngster exits the car with book bag in tow. So begins an all-important trust gap—the space between a promise made in the morning and the promise kept (or broken) in the afternoon. The level of anxiety the child experiences during the day depends on whether past experiences are more "Mom always comes" or "Sorry I'm late again; traffic was terrible."

We all live our lives on promises. From the time a child can grasp the concept of "cross my heart and hope to die," there is a forever realization that anxiety can be reduced only through proof of trust while waiting for a promise to be kept. From "Scout's honor" to "I do" to "the whole truth and nothing but the truth," we seek cues that allay our worries. Lifeguards, the bus schedule, and the spotlessness of a hospital room are all obvious artifacts of assurances.

The world of work has many forms of promises waiting to be kept. We recollect the evident power of trust when we see brand names that have attached guarantees to their offerings—FedEx, Domino's Pizza, Hampton Inn, Nordstrom, and L.L. Bean. And we sense its subtle power when the hotel finds our reservation, the newspaper is on the front porch, the bank statement is completely accurate, or mentors do exactly as they promise.

Protégés are exactly like the youth in this all-too-familiar story. Mentoring begins with a promise made or implied followed by a gap. The trust gap is the emotional space between hope and evidence, between expectation and fulfillment. Trust is the emotion that propels protégés to the other side of the gap. Insecurity and doubt are not required features of the trust gap. But requiring protégés to walk on the high wire of faith is clearly an inescapable component of every mentoring encounter. The journey across the high wire of faith is a trip with or without anguish, based only on the net of trust the mentor ensures is there to support passage.

There are many dimensions to managing the trust gap. A reputation as a promise keeper can help. Reminders can be communicated along the path that a promise made has not been forgotten. And there can be verbal and nonverbal cues that say to the protégé, "I am trustworthy—that is, worthy of your trust."

Mentoring: Steve Allen Style

Before Jay Leno there was host Johnny Carson. And before Johnny's long run, the host of *The Tonight Show* was Jack Paar. But before Jack, there was the very first host of the show in the mid-fifties—Steve Allen. Allen died in 2000 of an apparent heart attack at age 78 while napping at his son's home in Encino, California. The author of more than fifty books and five thousand songs, Steve Allen was regarded as the founding father of the late-night talk show. The world knew him as an accomplished comedian, talented musician, and innovative talk show host. But to the countless entertainers privileged to have been understudies to Allen—the late singer Andy Williams, actor and comedian Steve Martin, actor Billy Crystal, and the late actor Don Knotts—he was the consummate mentor.

The night following his death Larry King did a CNN special segment on the great Steve Allen. Admirers like *Tonight Show* co-host Ed McMahon, movie director Carl Reiner, and actor Mike Douglas were on the show. Call-ins included comedian Don Rickles and singer Andy Williams. Other interviews in print and on the air in the days that followed added to the epitaph crafted by King's guests by revealing the reason for Allen's huge fan club of entertainment greats. Allen had mentored them all with trust. All spoke of Allen's focus on them, not on himself.

Trust is a crucial commodity throughout a mentoring relationship. In fact, research shows that even if the mentor has terrific interpersonal skills, they count for naught without a high level of trust. Conversely, a mentor with only modest mentoring skills can be successful if the protégé experiences a high level of trust. But what is the nature of trust? If trust were something you could reverse-engineer, what parts would you find inside? Trust is a blend of authenticity (genuineness), credibility (reliability), and communication.

Communicating Genuineness, Allen-Style

Trust starts with authenticity. We trust another when we perceive his or her motives to be genuine or credible. And Steve Allen was always dramatically real! His assertive authenticity quickly calmed even the most uptight star-in-the-making. On one famous sketch on the forerunner of *The Tonight Show,* Allen got tickled at his own joke. The more he laughed, the more tickled he became. Instead of stopping to regain his composure, he simply let his honest giggle attack run rampant. It was unadulterated authenticity, expressed out loud. It counts among the funniest sketches in television history.

Although one of the most brilliant comedians in entertainment history, Allen always seemed awed by his capacity. He seemed so busy looking ahead at what he *could* be that he gave no time to gloating over what he *had been*. His fans and protégés say that his coaching conversations were more joint exploration than boasting exhibitions.

You're not a Steve Allen, you say? No matter. There are many ways you can demonstrate authenticity, especially at the beginning of the mentoring session. Start with a pleasant facial expression. Greet your protégé like you are sincerely glad to see him or her. Communicate your enthusiasm for the privilege of mentoring and what it can mean for both of you. Look for a way to provide an early honest compliment. And always remember two things: be completely honest, and never communicate in a manner that might be perceived by your protégé as patronizing. "You have a great reputation for being an enthusiastic learner" can be a much more powerful way to start building trust than "That sure is a handsome laptop case."

If you are feeling a bit anxious, say so—but in a fashion that helps build a bond. "I'm a bit overwhelmed by this mentoring assignment . . . but, at the same time I'm excited about what we can accomplish together" is much preferred to "I'm really nervous, are you?" Reveal something personal about yourself, especially something that your protégé may not know and that could provide insight into who you are. "I'm kind of a private person, and I may seem a bit hard to get to know at first" is much better than "I like baseball, Pabst Blue Ribbon® beer, and people who tell me what's on their mind. How about you?"

Communicating Credibility, Allen-Style

Trust depends on credibility. We trust another when we believe the person has the wherewithal to actually perform what is promised or needed. Wherewithal includes competence, credentials, and correct conduct. We examine the plaques on the physician's wall, see the badge on the police officer's uniform, or hear the tone of the pilot's voice during in-flight turbulence to gain clues into matters of credibility.

Allen was great at demonstrating credibility as a step in trust building. "What if we did it like this?" prefaced his lessons in stage performance. His tone carried three essential ingredients for communicating credibility: exposition, exploration, and inclusion. Allen knew how to show off without being a show-off. His display revealed the edge of his enormous talent in a fashion that gave his protégé a kind of "this guy is really good" confidence in him without unleashing an intimidating internal reaction of "I could never do that." His lessons were "we" lessons, as in "a smart person mentoring a smart person." "He was always willing to share what he knew," said Ed McMahon, "as if it was yours all along and he was simply returning something he had borrowed."

How does a mentor communicate credibility without alienating or intimidating the protégé? Credibility needs to fit the context, and the mentoring context is one of support and partnership. A boxing coach might gain credibility with a demeanor as clipped and gruff as an upper cut. The credibility context for a surgeon might be more factual than illustrative, grounded more in technique than in rapport. But in the business world, credibility is best expressed more subtly—in the way one might add a pinch of salt to a bland dish. Credibility should enter the relationship as if somehow invited by the protégé, not sent by the mentor.

Tell a personal story that uses your expertise as the backdrop, not the subject. "When I was helping Stan Dupp craft his strategic plan, we faced the dilemma of how to get the enthusiastic endorsement of the union." Preface an affirmation with a small tidbit from your resume. "Your new role sounds as exciting as the regional VP slot I had in South Africa in '88!" Keep in mind, the intent is to reveal, not brag. A boasting attitude will shift the spotlight onto you, not your protégé. Share a take-away that benefits the protégé but trumpets your competence or eligibility. "You might find this white paper I wrote helpful in explaining some of the craziness of this industry." Ask questions that reveal expertise but never in a testing manner or egotistical fashion. Remember, credibility is a tool for trust—your protégé's trust! Consider your exposition of your talents from the perspective of what your protégé needs, not what you need.

Communicating Anything, Allen-Style

Trust comes in part through communication that contains two features: *task* (underscore precision and authority) and *personal* (emphasis on empathy and consideration). When someone speaks with noticeable authority and crystal clarity, our trust meter goes up. When someone tries to communicate with us with our welfare obviously in mind, she or he gains our confidence. Interpersonal trust is by definition both personal and interpersonal—as in "between persons." And the link we have between persons is our manner of communication.

Steve Allen was a master at both aspects of trust-building communication. His booming voice could be heard across a crowded party. And being well over six feet tall didn't hurt his projection prowess. But it was his purity of purpose that latchkeyed attention. "He was a man who spoke with conviction," said his protégé Andy Williams. "When he spoke, people listened because he not only knew what he was talking about, he *sounded* like he knew what he was talking about." When he invited his audiences to give him a subject on which he would craft a song on the spot, he got plenty of volunteers. Audiences knew that his confident requests not only telegraphed his assurance but also would lead to their amusement, not to feeding his arrogance.

When you talk with your protégé, think of it as trust-building communication that increases in cost with each nonessential word you use ... verbosity is expensive; brevity is cost-effective. Focus on being precise and particular. That's the task element in gaining trust. But here is the equally important part: as you subtract syllables, add expressions of kindness. Trust is just as much about communicating sincere interest in your protégé as it is about scrupulous attention to clarity.

When offering advice or feedback, keep your suggestions crisp and obvious; speak with the confidence of your experience. When getting feedback from your protégé, be quickly appreciative and bold in unearthing additional learning; show confidence in your ability to transform even negative observations into an opportunity for growth. It is the centeredness a sage might communicate to a student, the peacefulness a tutor might convey to a new pupil.

Steve Allen's genius lies not in the archives of his many TV sketches or the books and music that line library walls. It lives on in the many famous entertainers who reflect his tutelage. When the late Andy Williams crooned *Moon River,* or scaredy-cat Don Knotts stammered, "But, but, but, Andy ... ," or Steve Lawrence and Eydie Gorme sang, *Our Love Is Here to Stay*, a little bit of Steve Allen shone through. And mentors who learn to build trust Allen-style are likewise blessed by his legacy.

7

The Person in the Mirror
Mentor Humility Creates Protégé Confidence

I bid him look into the lives of men as though into a mirror, and from others to take an example for himself.

Terence (190–159 BC)

This chapter was written by Marshall Goldsmith.

As a Ph.D student at UCLA in the early 1970s, I had a self-image of being "hip" and "cool." I believed I was intensely involved in deep human understanding, self-actualization, and the uncovering of profound wisdom. Early in my Ph.D program, I was one of thirteen students in a class led by a wise teacher, Bob Tannenbaum. Bob had come up with the term "sensitivity training," had published the most widely distributed article to appear in the *Harvard Business Review*, and was a full professor. He was an important person in our department at UCLA.

In Bob's class, we were encouraged to discuss anything we wanted to discuss. I began by talking about people in Los Angeles. For three full weeks I gave monologues about how "screwed up" people in Los Angeles were. "They wear those $78 sequined blue jeans and drive gold Rolls Royces; they are plastic and materialistic; all they care about is impressing others; and they really do not understand what is deep and important in life." (It was easy for me to be an expert on the people of Los Angeles. I had, after all, grown up in a small town in Kentucky.)

One day, after listening to me babble for three weeks, Bob looked at me quizzically and asked, "Marshall, who are you talking to?"

"I am speaking to the group," I answered.

"Who in the group are you talking to?"

"Well, I am talking to everybody," I replied, not quite knowing where he was headed with this line of questioning.

"I don't know if you realize this," Bob said, "but each time you have spoken, you have looked at only one person. You have addressed your comments toward only one person. And you seem interested in the opinion of only one person. Who is that person?"

"That is interesting. Let me think about it," I replied. Then (after careful consideration) I said, "You?"

He said, "That's right, me. There are twelve other people in this room. Why don't you seem interested in any of them?"

Now that I had dug myself into a hole, I decided to dig even deeper. I said, "You know, Dr. Tannenbaum, I think you can understand the true significance of what I am saying. I think you can truly understand how 'screwed up' it is to try to run around and impress people all the time. I believe you have a deep understanding of what is really important in life."

Bob looked at me and said, "Marshall, is there any chance that for the last three weeks all you have been trying to do is impress me?"

I was amazed at Bob's obvious lack of insight! "Not at all!" I declared. "I don't think you have understood one thing I have said! I have been explaining to you how 'screwed up' it is to try to impress other people. I think you have totally missed my point, and frankly, I am a little disappointed in your lack of understanding!"

He looked at me, scratched his beard, and concluded, "No, I think I understand."

I looked around and saw twelve people scratching their faces and thinking, "Yes. We understand."

Suddenly, I had a deep dislike for Dr. Tannenbaum. I devoted a lot of energy to figuring out his psychological problems and understanding why he was confused. But after six months, it finally dawned on me that the person with the issue wasn't him. It wasn't even the people in Los Angeles. The person with the real issue was me. I finally looked in the mirror and said, "You know, old Dr. Tannenbaum was exactly right."

Two of the greatest lessons I began to understand from this experience were (1) that it is much easier to see our problems in others than it is to see them in ourselves, and (2) even though we may be able to deny our problems to ourselves, they may be very obvious to the people who are observing us.

There is almost always a discrepancy between the self we think we are and the self the rest of the world sees in us. The lesson I learned (and strive in my professional work to help others understand) is that often the rest of the world has a more accurate perspective than we do. If we can stop, listen, and think about what others see in us, we have a great opportunity. We can compare the self that we want to be with the self we are presenting to the rest of the world. We can then begin to make the real changes needed to align our stated values with our actual values.

I have told this story at least three hundred times, and I have thought about it more frequently than I have told it. Often when I become self-righteous, preachy, holier-than-thou, or angry about some perceived injustice, I eventually realize that the issue is not with the other person or people. The issue is usually me.

Today I work mostly with executives in large organizations. I help them develop a profile of desired leadership behavior. Then I provide them with confidential feedback, which allows them to compare their behavior (as perceived by others) with their profile of desired behavior. I try to help them deal with this feedback in a positive way, to learn from it, and (eventually) to become a good role model for the desired leadership behavior in their organization. Although I am supposed to be a "coach," very little of my coaching involves "sharing my wisdom." Most of it involves helping my clients learn from the people around them. In this way, the lesson I learned from Bob Tannenbaum has not only helped me in my personal life; it has helped shape the course of my professional life.

8

Inside the Mind
of the Protégé
When Fear and Learning Collide

Education is the ability to listen to almost anything without losing your temper or your self-confidence.

Robert Frost

Fear is as personal as a fingerprint. We have a daredevil friend whose idea of a fun Saturday afternoon is to bungee jump off a bridge or skydive from a helicopter. The thought of either makes us break out in a cold sweat. What frightens one person is another person's playground.

Understanding the protégé's emotional state, particularly at the start of the relationship, is an essential first step of creating an atmosphere of acceptance and trust. Keep in mind that fear is far more a liability than an asset where learning is involved. A testing, contentious learning environment may bring out the adrenaline but does not bolster aptitude. Learners who are fearful tend to take fewer risks. And protégés differ in what elevates their anxiety. What is the physiology of fear, and how can that knowledge serve mentors?

Let's take a deep dive into the mind of the protégé—especially

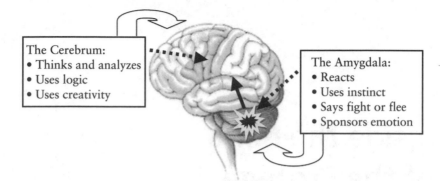

The Cerebrum:
• Thinks and analyzes
• Uses logic
• Uses creativity

The Amygdala:
• Reacts
• Uses instinct
• Says fight or flee
• Sponsors emotion

Figure 2. The Human Brain's Cerebrum and Amygdala

one at the most anxious end of the fear continuum. We begin with a review of what you probably learned in ninth-grade general science or tenth-grade biology about the workings of the brain. The brain is divided into many parts. We will focus on two key parts—the cerebrum and the amygdala (see Figure 2). The cerebrum is that big gray wrinkly part that we typically call the brain. It is divided into two halves (or hemispheres)—the right side is the intuitive, creative or emotional side; the left is the logical, analytical or rational side.

What does the cerebrum do? In its entirety it is the seat of logic, creativity, analysis, insight, learning, and problem solving. We humans have the largest cerebrum in relation to body weight of any species. In fact, the label *Homo sapiens* comes from the Latin meaning "wise or knowing man."

And the amygdala? From an evolutionary perspective, it is one of the oldest parts of the brain and controls instinct and a person's physical reaction to danger. Sometimes referred to as the reptilian brain (or, with a hat tip to Seth Godin, the lizard brain), it controls the fight-or-flight response and triggers the secretion of adrenaline—the hormone that gets dumped into the bloodstream to make us faster, stronger, and tougher when threatened. Adrenaline is not stored in the brain, but it is the amygdala that flips the switch causing its release. It is what makes your hair stand on end and enables all your senses to be much sharper and keener in a crisis.

When you experience anything in life, imagine the message taking two routes. The slower route goes to the cerebrum; the faster route goes to the amygdala (see Figure 2). The amygdala is connected to the cerebrum and acts much like an early-warning clearinghouse for any signs of threat. If the amygdala senses danger, it quickly sends a message to the cerebrum requesting it to ignore the forthcoming message (the slower-moving information). With that warning, the cerebrum mostly shuts down—sometimes as much as two-thirds of it—in order to allow the amygdala to deal with the threat situation in a reactive or instinctive way. In other words, evolution has enabled the brain to let instinct rule over logic in times of threat or danger.

Imagine a caveman out on a leisurely stroll when he suddenly encounters a mean, angry saber-toothed tiger. If the caveman thought to himself, "Let me figure this out. Seems to me I recall my father telling me if I saw one of these animals I needed to move to the left, no wait, I believe it was move to the right," what do you think would happen? He'd be lunch to the tiger. So the brain learned that in saber-toothed tiger situations, we will live longer if the situation is dealt with instinctively and reactively rather than logically and rationally.

The brain works today much like it did then. Actually, today it is not the threat of physical harm that triggers the amygdala's taking over for the cerebrum; it is the threat of emotional harm, which can range in severity from mild disappointment to downright fury. The more the sense of harm moves to the fury end, the more "victim" the protégé feels. The path to getting a good connection is to remember the protégé is not acting rationally but acting threatened.

What does being a victim really mean to a protégé? It could mean many things to a protégé: "I will appear stupid"; "I will lose composure or control"; "My embarrassment will be obvious"; "My mentor will harm my reputation"; "I will lose now but I'll lose even more next time." You get the idea.

The point is, when people go into this state, they are not operating out of their normal thinking brain. They are operating out of the world of fight-or-flight—they want to fight or flee. Since in the typical mentoring relationship, a fight (arguing, blaming, resisting, etc.) is not deemed an appropriate response, the protégé will opt to flee. This might not be literally running out of the room; it will more likely be reserve, extreme shyness, noticeable timidity, and posture that spells "defense."

The most important point is that higher-level learning (as opposed to instinctive or rote learning like someone might use in boot camp) is acquired in the cerebrum (now dormant) rather than the amygdala, now in charge. The goal of rapport building is to invite the protégés out of their "terror" state to a more rational state where effective learning (a.k.a., risk taking) can occur.

Partners Soothe

Imagine you are the parent of a small child who wakes up in the middle of the night frightened by a bad dream. In tears, the child comes into your bedroom. What would you do and say? The answer is easy—you would model bravery and confidence; you would carefully listen without judgment; and you would offer great empathy as you seek to calm and encourage. The principles used for a small child with a bad dream are the same for protégés in a state of anxiety.

Scared protégés feel victimized in some way. The source of the fear may vary. We all have our hot-button triggers hardwired to early experiences and learnings, albeit sometimes causing irrational beliefs. Regardless of what's driving the protégé's sense of victimization, the response should demonstrate the complete absence or even hint of threat. The attitude of the mentor should always be one that reflects calm and confidence. A calm attitude will help to reflect humility and the attitude you want from the protégé. A confident attitude will soothe because in the tense early stages of mentoring you want the protégé to know you are confidently there for him or her.

Another essential in partner-like soothing is **humility,** our label for sincere compassion, authentic concern, and total vulnerability. Humility is crucial in the mentor's response to a scared protégé because it communicates "I am not your enemy." It announces a kind of no-fight-or-flee zone in order to calm the anxious protégé out of the "ready to flee" amygdala-driven mode. It begins with creating a connection that demonstrates sincere interest and obvious concern. Use open posture and eye contact. Listen to the protégé and, equally important, look as if you are listening. The tone chosen is equally important. Again, model the attitude you would like the protégé to assume. Let the protégé witness your genuine interest and concern.

Partners Understand

It is important to remember that before you can engage in facilitating insight, you must get the protégés out of the part of the brain they are currently in (the amygdala) and into the part of the brain where learning and discovery occur (the cerebrum). The amygdala is telling them to get ready to flee or fight. The actions of the mentor need to signal that the protégé's defensive stance is not necessary. Humility begins to set the stage, but it is the search for understanding that causes the protégé to shift from the frightened posture to a receptive and accepting mode.

Empathy is an expression of kinship and a powerful partnering practice. It says to the protégé you are like the protégé—not above or below. It means using words that communicate complete identification with the protégé, that you fully appreciate the impact the fear of the unknown has on him. It is like saying, "I get it! I know just how uncomfortable this is. I am in tune with where you are, and I would feel just like you do if I were entering a relationship like this one."

It is important to show confidence while demonstrating empathy. In other words, it is inappropriate for the mentor to wallow in bad feelings. Remember, empathy is not synonymous with sympathy.

Your protégé does not need someone to cry with (sympathy or shared weakness); he wants an understanding shoulder to cry on (empathy or the gift of strength). Empathy communicates understanding and identification. It means listening to learn, not listening to make a point or to correct. Deal with feelings before you deal with facts.

Partners Bolster Self-Esteem

Let's assume you now have a clearer understanding of the person. What's next? The first thing you can do is to pay attention to the nuances, the subtle cues, the subtext of your discussions with your protégé—anything that might signal some fear that needs to be addressed. Then, answer the literal words of a question while you address the deeper issue that you think might be fueling the protégé's fear.

You also can play a major role in bolstering the protégé's low self-esteem and thus help to push fear out. Mentors do not *give* courage, they *uncover* courage. Two ways you can help the protégé find hidden courage are:

- **Use lots of positive affirmations!** Mentors sometimes approach protégés as though affirmations are rare and expensive gifts to be doled out parsimoniously. Somewhere they heard that too much praise would make a protégé lazy. This is a sad fallacy. William James, the great psychologist-philosopher, said it well: "The deepest craving of humans is the need to be appreciated." Look for things to compliment; lavish praise with sincerity and enthusiasm.

- **Assume that the protégé has no reason for low self-esteem.** This means never buying into a protégé's low opinion of himself. Although this may sound harsh, it can be a powerful gift. This subtle message in the mentor's attitude will become self-fulfilling and in time help the protégé let go of the old self-view and assume a new feeling of worth. You may have seen the classic play and film *My Fair Lady*. Professor Henry Higgins wanted to see whether he could take a lowly flower girl from the streets of London and train her so well that he could pass her off as a member of the nobility at an upper-crust ball. As Eliza Doolittle learned the ways and speech of an aristocratic lady, she became one.

Fear is a barrier to learning. When protégés bring fear into a learning environment, they limit the depth and breadth of their growth. Great mentors are fear hunters. Invite your protégé to hunt fear with you, and together enjoy the bounty of your success.

9

Fail Faster

Interview with Liz Smith,
Chairman of the Board of Directors
and CEO of Bloomin' Brands

How would you characterize or describe your most important mentor?

My most important professional mentor is Irene Rosenfeld, chairman and CEO of Kraft Foods. I worked with her at Kraft over the course of my fourteen years there. With Irene, what you see is what you get. She never has a personal agenda. She's smart, objective, and fair-dealing. She is also a very courageous leader. She's not afraid to put any truth on the table, no matter what it looks like. She always operates with transparency.

What were the traits you found most instrumental in your mentor's work with you?

When I first worked with Irene, I was a brand manager, and she came into the Desserts Division as the division president. There were many levels between us. At the time, the Desserts Division was struggling, and she was brought in to turn it around. Irene values a flat organization. By that, I mean she makes herself accessible and wants to hear from everyone in the organization to better understand what is going on. Although I was still just a brand manager, I spent a lot of time with her discussing the business and what I thought the issues were. This was the first time I'd seen a division manager at that level work so far down in the organization to make sure she had a read on the business, that she knew the people, that she was current. She is what I call a "level-less" leader. She doesn't communicate through hierarchy or bureaucracy. I felt like (1) I could tell her the truth about what was happening. I didn't have to spin anything. And (2) I knew she would listen. This made a big impression on me, and has always stayed with me. In every job I've had, I've made sure that I had a strong connection at every level in the organization.

What is one example or incident or illustration of how this person was helpful to you?

When Irene took over as head of Kraft North America businesses, we were having our challenges like every other company. But there was a politeness to Kraft—it's a very Midwest kind of culture with great values but too much hierarchy and formality. People would often talk around issues and be polite instead of talking more directly about challenges. I was a division manager at that point, so I was pretty senior. Irene called all of the division managers together; between all of us we represented about $30–40 billion in business. I'll never forget the slide she put up to start our meeting. The title of the slide was "Things Heard in the Halls of Kraft Foods." On the slide were all the topics and issues that people were really thinking about but not saying about the business, about the culture, and what needed to change.

She completely disarmed the group. She literally dragged out every single skeleton that might be in any closet. She said, "We can't change what we can't own and acknowledge. You are the senior leaders of this organization. This is what people are talking about but not telling us. We're going to have to own this." A big sigh went through the room and we got to work with more candor on the real issues. This invitation to be transparent was real leadership courage.

What advice or feedback did this person provide that was helpful to you?

Irene once said to me, "Liz, it's okay to fail, but you have to fail faster." I use that line all the time now. She told me, "You have great business instincts. Listen to them. I bet you knew that this project was not going as you thought it would a long time before you put the red flag up. It's okay to fail, but have the courage to call an audible if something that you've created or are leading isn't going the way it should." It is such great advice and so true. A lot of times people are afraid and don't listen to that little voice that says, "Wait a minute." They keep chasing after something because they're invested in it, personally or professionally—versus just saying, "It's not what I thought, and we're going to cut bait and fail faster."

ACCEPTING—CREATING A SAFE HAVEN FOR RISK TAKING

Pope John XXIII was probably the most beloved pope in recent history. The devotion people felt for him was due in part to the fact that he was completely without pretense. His openness and humility endeared him to millions, Catholic and non-Catholic alike. One of his first official acts was to visit the prisoners in a large penal institution in Rome. As he gave the inmates his blessing, he shared with them the fact that he had been in a prison, too—to visit his cousin!

Sidney Jourard, in his classic, *The Transparent Self,* describes countless research studies demonstrating conclusively that humans have a natural, built-in tendency to be open and revealing.[1] When that tendency is thwarted, the individual reacts by becoming closed, cautious, and reserved. The longer this blockage occurs, the more difficult it is for trusting relationships to develop. In his book *Why Am I Afraid to Tell You Who I Am?* John Powell answers his title

91

question, "Because if I tell you who I am, you may not like who I am, and it's all that I have."[2]

In the last few chapters we explored different dimensions of the core competency and first step in the mentoring process: *surrendering*. In Part 3 we will examine the second crucial core competency of great mentoring: *accepting*. Accepting is evaluation-free, egalitarian encountering—mentoring without arrogance, bias, prejudice, or selectivity.

Accepting means inviting the learner to be courageous, to take the risks needed to unfreeze old habits, and to embrace and internalize new practices. This entails sending all manner of signals and signs that hearten the learner to boldness and provide support, despite unstable first attempts and timid trials. The mentor's willingness to act in ways that are noticeably gallant is a part of that invitational signaling process. Such actions say to the protégé, "I value you enough to accept you despite your imperfections." Think of it as a human form of grace. (Grace among some religious groups means "undeserved forgiveness.")

Mentors who are effective at demonstrating acceptance also foster a spirit of inquiry on a level emotional playing field—a relationship with unrestricted access, from which all issues unrelated to learning are barred. They reveal a riveting curiosity in the protégé through their dramatic listening, empathetic inquiry, and productive dialogue. When mentors listen to learn (not to instruct), when mentors question to unearth (not to prove), and when mentors converse to explore (not to boast or best), the protégé experiences acceptance. The next five chapters focus on skills and techniques that support competence in accepting. This part begins with the most crucial accepting skill—encouraging courage.

10

Invitations to Risk
Acceptance as a Nurturer of Courage

When we see that to learn, we must be willing to look foolish, to let another teach us, learning doesn't always look so good anymore.... Only with the support and fellowship of another can we face the dangers of learning meaningful things.

Peter Senge

Learning can be a scary proposition. The protégé's path is not only potentially embarrassing, awkward, and unpleasant; it generally comes with no guarantee of success. And learning in its rawest form almost always entails a public display of weakness. Learning without entry into the dis-comfort zone is not likely to be true learning. No one learns to walk without falling a lot, and higher levels of learning are no different. Learning without facing some chance of failure is superficial progress, not real, integrated change.

Learners are brave pioneers. They leave a comfortable, safe "who I am" in search of an unknown, vulnerable "who I can be." They are willing to withstand emotional "arrows in the back" as they blaze unfamiliar territory, abandoning a space of inner security to engage in temporary recklessness. They boldly take steps knowing skinned knees (and egos) are in the offing. There is a sort of an emotional masochism at play when an imagined benefit

93

outweighs established certainty and the learner deliberately plunges into a realm of probable anxiety. What can a mentor do to support such pioneering recklessness? What can a mentor do to stir learner bravery? How can mentors guide protégés to take responsible risks?

Courage is not an attribute or quality to be bestowed, despite our language to the contrary. We don't really *give* courage, as if it is something one imparts or donates to another. Instead, think of courage as a preexisting condition, there to be awakened. Like a shy child on the fringe of a noisy party, courage is a trait that is already present but in need of an invitation to "join the fun." The role of mentor is to partner with the protégé to surface courage and then to support the protégé in recognizing its presence. Acceptance is the context in which that surfacing and supporting occur.

Acceptance entails actions that communicate unconditional positive regard. Acceptance is confirmation without concurrence. It says, "I value you even if I disagree with you or disapprove of your actions." Acceptance is a living announcement of worth. It is communicating the sentiment contained in Mary Haskell's quote: "Nothing you become will disappoint me.... I have no desire to foresee you, only to discover you. You can't disappoint me." In a mentoring partnership, it is an invitation to risk, extended to the protégé in three ways: dynamic modeling, judgment-free communication, and rational affirmation.

Invitation # 1: Dynamic modeling

"Leaders are much more powerful role models when they learn than when they teach," says Harvard Business School professor Rosabeth Moss Kanter. There is no more effective teaching technique than personal example. If you are inviting the protégé to take risks and you also engage in risk taking, you are communicating acceptance. Courage hidden will join courage displayed. Remember our analogy of courage being like a shy child at a party? A public request by the host of the party for all shy children to join in the fun is not likely to invoke participation. But, if another child makes a private, personal but determined invitation, the outcome will be completely different.

The modeling of courage needs to be dynamic, not subtle. Dynamic modeling means you act as an obvious prototype for the protégé. Courage building requires far more than cheerleading support from the sidelines. And this is no time to try to let nuance and nicety carry the day. Dynamic modeling requires "Follow me!" behavior that is obvious and noticeable. Why? A protégé's reluctance to be bold is sometimes fueled by the absence of a "show how it's done" example.

"I read this great article on... ," "I met with Sue because I knew she could teach me how to... ," and "The course I'm taking online has helped me to..."—all are examples of dynamic modeling that telegraph two things: an allegiance to continuous learning and an enthusiastic participation in the process. Your goal is not to model being a fan of learning. Your goal is to model being a learner—and a passionate one! Help your learning actions get up on a table and shout!

Take your protégé to a seminar, conference, or workshop—anywhere you can learn together. Take a webinar together. Ask your protégé to teach you something she or he knows that you'd like to learn. If you attend a conference or seminar, make time to share with your protégé the highlights of your learning and what you plan to do with your newfound knowledge. If your protégé attends a seminar, class, webinar, or conference, schedule time to pick his or her brain afterwards. Celebrate people who boldly pursue growth—the clerk who finishes a degree after several years' interlude, the supervisor who tutors after hours, or the operator who writes an article for a local trade magazine.

End meetings by soliciting suggestions for improvement on how to make the next meeting better. Invite unique people to attend—people who offer a point of view or perspective that can challenge, provoke, and inspire. Keep a "sages on call" list—inventors, artists, writers, anyone who can provide new ways of seeing challenges, attacking problems, or inventing solutions.

Invitation # 2: Judgment-Free Communication

Anatomy experts tell us that courage occurs physiologically when the circuits in the thinking portion of the brain—the cerebral cortex—turn on and restrain or curb the overexcited emotional center of the brain. This means that rather than being emotionally stymied, clear thinking directs action even in the face of risks.

Mentors see the opportunities for collective exploration as chances to make good even better. Focusing on their role as the conveyor of wisdom, mentors have a confident view and see no minefields of emotional loss. However, protégés enter collective exploration looking up at a setting filled with the possibility for failure. In their mind's eye they witness extremely foolish comments and grossly disappointing faux pas. They believe that somehow their hidden inadequacies—ones they view as massive—will suddenly be exposed and come under the disapproving scrutiny of a critical judge. Weighed by this exaggerated perception of reality, hearts race, memories halt, and the entire speaking apparatus is abruptly inoperative... and bone dry!

This is where nonjudgmental communication works as a magical antidote. Instead of a tone of censure, great mentors communicate the warmth of acceptance. An open posture replaces the cross-armed stare a protégé might anticipate. Their pace is slow and deliberate, not clipped and ambiguous. Gestures are invitational and affirming, not negative and tentative. Nonjudgmental communication uses nonthreatening expressions such as "What were your reasons for...?" instead of "Why did you...?"

Above all, nonjudgmental communication works by sending a friendly message that the protégé's emotional armor is unnecessary and can be discarded. The key is to make the message an act of discovery—based on the idea that the protégé's view is completely legitimate and normal, but also inaccurate. This is best done by refraining from commenting on the protégé's nervousness directly. Instead, talk with the protégé as if anxiety were nowhere in sight. It is also important to use some self-effacing "I'm just like you" comments or examples. Mentor vulnerability is a powerful tool in dissipating protégé fear.

Invitation # 3: Rational Affirmation

Ever thought about the role of cheering at an athletic event? We don't watch in silence. But neither are our shouts of pleasure when our favorite team is winning like the sounds we might make if we sank a hole in one or won the sweepstakes. Cheering is not simply an expression of joy but also one of affirmation. Our intent is to encourage, support, and coax. When sports announcers speak of the "home field advantage," they are acknowledging the power of affirmation as a tool for summoning courage.

"Rational affirmation" is an intentional oxymoron. Remember, evoking courage is about quieting the overactive, irrational anxiety in the protégé. Flattering the protégé with some schmaltzy, generalized "Attaboy!" will surely be considered patronizing. The protégé is likely to be thinking, "You clearly see my foibles and are just trying to be nice to me." The goal is to communicate in a form that is accurate and clear (like the football versions of "Go defense!") yet sunny in its nature. Affirmations should be straightforward ("You ask very good questions that make me see things in a new way") and never contrived or backhanded.

An effective mentor invites the protégé to face the risks of learning by being a good model, engaging in judgment-free communication, and offering rational (i.e., believable) affirmation. When the protégé witnesses courage, hears the sound of courage, and feels the glow of courage, experimentation ensues and wisdom results.

11

Socrates' Great Secret

Awesome Queries

Judge a man by his questions rather than his answers.

Voltaire

If there were a Mentors' Hall of Fame, Socrates would be an instant inductee. In a heated argument over whether slaves have souls (the ancient Greeks believed that only smart people would have eternal life), Socrates bet a case of mead (no doubt Greek for Bud Light) that he could teach a common slave the Pythagorean theorem (for those who used it in high school and then filed it away: the square of the hypotenuse of a right triangle is equal to the sum of the squares of the other two sides). He had no PowerPoint slides, handouts, or textbook. He needed only two tools to teach the slave: the capacity to ask the right question and the ability to listen carefully to the meaning behind the answer. To this day the method behind his bold bet is memorialized as Socratic teaching.

Socrates understood the secret of mentoring: effective questioning brings insight, which fuels curiosity, which cultivates wisdom. Now we will examine, methodically and anecdotally, how the Socratic method works. You will learn why Socrates' secret is such a powerful one.

Quality questions have a multiplier effect on learning. Ask an information-seeking question and you get only an answer or a fact; ask an understanding-seeking question and you unleash a more powerful chain of events. Here's how it works.

The Creative Human Computer

The human brain is often compared to a computer, but it is actually very different. Most computers are largely information-storage devices. Ask an information-seeking question, and the computer goes into a retrieval mode—as does the human brain. However, ask an understanding-seeking question, and the mind has to make up an answer not found in the storage closet of the brain. Computers cannot make up answers. Understanding-seeking questions stimulate the kind of mental activity that creates insight or discovery. As the mind leaps and turns and twists to respond to an understanding-seeking question, special new synapses are activated and the insight experience occurs.

"Insight is the brain at play," brain researcher Pierce Howard, author of *The Owner's Manual for the Brain,* told us recently, "and the brain loves to play."[1] Discovery—that "Aha!" experience of finding a connection, closing a gap, or completing a pattern—is very rewarding to the mind. So rewarding, in fact, that the mind is constantly on the lookout for an opportunity to repeat the experience. And the more "Aha!"s the mind gets, the hungrier the mind is for them. Finding information is easy and boring; crafting understanding is challenging and exhilarating. The more the mind experiences creative discovery, the more the mind hunts another insight. This pursuit of insight or discovery is what we call "curiosity." To the mind, curiosity is its own reward. And the by-product of perpetual curiosity is wisdom.

How to Ask Questions

A friend of ours had a little run-in with the state highway patrol. It started with being stopped and ended with a traffic ticket. But the question in the middle made all the difference between a super-positive experience and one he would like to forget. But we will let him tell the story.

"I admit I was driving 70 mph! It was a bright Sunday morning and I was driving on a four-lane highway in a rural area with not a car on the road. Without warning (and without any change in the setting), the speed limit sign dropped the limit to 45 mph. I missed it. It was obviously some local small town's way of funding their budget—a speed trap with the speed limit sign. But instead of the local sheriff, I met a state highway patrol car. When he suddenly slowed, crossed the medium and quickly pursued me, I realized the error of my ways and pulled to the shoulder. I withdrew my license and insurance proof and waited for my 'whoopin'!

"The officer reviewed my identification and calmly asked, 'Mr. Smith, is there an emergency I need to know about?' I was flabbergasted! Instead of the anticipated, 'Do you realize how fast you were driving?' I got a sincere, nonjudgmental assumption that an emergency must be what was driving my decision to drive 25 mph above the posted speed limit. The officer was polite and courteous . . . and above all, confident. And the impact on me? I was completely honest about the error of my ways and he wrote out my speeding ticket that carried a hefty fine. Guess what? I wrote a thank you note to the state highway patrol department, specifically complimenting this officer."

How does the mentor start this insight-curiosity-wisdom chain? One major chain starter is the understanding-seeking question. Great mentors, aware that their objective is to foster wisdom, are skilled at asking these questions. Below are several important techniques for crafting and asking questions that produce insight.

Assessing Your Inquiry Talents

The Mentor Scale can be a helpful tool in examining your talents and blind spots with regard to inquiry. Below are a few things to watch out for, tied to the scoring form you completed in Chapter 3.

Sociability

Low: Watch out for too much silence. If the protégé does not answer in ten seconds, she may need you to redirect the question. Also, know that eye contact can be important in conveying a sincere interest in the protégé's answers. Tape your conversations to self-evaluate your style of inquiry.

High: Beware of not giving the protégé an opportunity to answer. Silence can be golden. Pause after asking a question. If you are susceptible to this trap, count to ten after asking a question and before asking another or rephrasing the one you just asked. Assume that the protégé heard and understood and is simply contemplating an answer.

Dominance

Low: Think before you ask. You may tend to let the interaction wander by asking questions just to ask questions. Consider your goal and focus. Determine what you seek to learn, then choose questions that will take you there.

Start with a Setup Statement

This may seem strange, but the best way to ask an insight-producing question is to start with a statement. Here's the reason: questions can be more powerful if the sender and receiver are clearly on the same wavelength—and know that they are. Starting with a setup statement establishes identification and context. It creates a milieu that makes the follow-up question much more powerful.

Mentor: (Setup) Jan, you've been working for about eight weeks now on the Dunn review.

Protégé: (Answer) That's right. I've had to put in some long hours on it.

High: You may have a tendency to craft questions that give you the answer you like to hear. Leading the protégé is just as inappropriate and ineffective as leading the witness. Soften your tone; make sure your approach does not make the protégé feel as though he were on trial.

Openness

Low: Avoid keeping your questions too much on the surface. While invading privacy is not the goal, your aim is to foster in-depth thinking. Be willing to allow a bit of controversy; conflict is nothing more than a symptom of tension. When you accurately interpret and work through conflict by your candor and openness, interpersonal closeness and valuable creativity will be the likely by-products.

High: You may often find yourself wanting to answer for the protégé. Back off and give the person a chance to communicate her thoughts. It is also important to avoiding getting too personal too quickly. While you may be more than ready to foster closeness, the protégé may need a bit more time.

Mentor: (Question) What have you learned about the project that you didn't expect to learn?

Notice how much more effective the question is after the mentor first makes a statement to establish identification (I am on your wavelength) and context (We have now established what area we are focusing on). It communicates to the protégé, "I've done my homework, I care, I'm eager to learn with you." It also helps the protégé to focus cleanly on the question and not on establishing a background to shore up the answer. Imagine how defensive the question alone might make the protégé feel.

Ask Questions that Require Higher-Level Thinking

Remember that the ultimate goal is to create insight, not to share information. Granted, some information sharing may be necessary; the main objective, however, is to nurture understanding and growth, not just exchange facts. Construct questions that require the protégé to dig deep to answer. Questions that force *comparisons* can accomplish this: "What are ways the Hollar project was different from the Dickinson project?" Questions that require *synthesis* can induce deeper thinking: "What do you see as the key implications of Mr. Rivers's assessment?" And questions that call for *evaluation* can provoke higher-level thinking: "If you could handle that assignment again, what would you do differently?"

The conventional wisdom on questioning has always been to ask open-ended questions. Closed questions, the lesson goes, will cause the receiver to deliver a short, single-word or single-phrase answer. However, the process is more complex than that. Socrates'sunderstanding-seeking questions did not just make the slave talk—they made him think. Anyone with a teenager knows that the answers to questions beginning with "what," "how," and "why" can be as short as those for a yes-no question. The intent of questioning to seek understanding is not just more words in the answer but more depth in the thinking needed to produce the answer.

Avoid Questions that Begin with "Why?"

Why avoid "why" questions? The point was made earlier, but it bears repeating. In most cultures, a sentence that begins with the word "why" and ends in a question mark is usually perceived as judgmental and indicting. Granted, body language can play a role in how such questions are perceived, but even with perfect body language, our antennae go up as soon as we hear a "why" question.

Find ways to soften the interrogatory question. "Why did you do that?" can sound very different from "What were your reasons for doing that?" The word "why" is not the problem; it is putting "why" on the front of a question. As we learned earlier, judgment can turn an open atmosphere into one of protection, caution, and guarded behavior. Without vulnerability there is no risk; without risk there is no experimentation and growth.

Use Curiosity to Stimulate Curiosity

Socrates did more than ask good questions. Socrates demonstrated an enthusiasm for the learning process. He believed in it and was excited to participate in demonstrating it. Attitude is as much a part of the Socratic method as technique.

A few years ago, stereographic pictures became the rage. People stared at them for long periods, trying to find the image or object among what seemed a random mixture of colored dots. A teenage girl in a shopping mall helped her boyfriend "see" a picture she had earlier figured out. The girl and boy were equally curious, both eager for the image to be discovered again, both excited when the insight finally came to him. Mentoring is like that.

Great mentors are not only curious; they are excited by the opportunity to stimulate other people's curiosity. Their attitude is "I can't wait to see the lights come on for you!" They are open about their excitement and verbally communicate pleasure when the protégé's "Aha!" finally comes.

Take stock of the greatest mentors down through the ages—Jesus, Buddha, Moses, Mohammed, Confucius, to name a few. Their influence was due in part to their ability to challenge their learners with thought-provoking questions. The same is true of modern mentors. In a study done a few years ago, Fortune 500 CEOs were asked what contributed most to their success.[2] Many listed an effective mentor as one of the key factors. To the question of what made these important people so influential, the most common response harkened back to mead and Socrates: "They asked great questions." Questions are the jewels of mentoring.

12

The Ear of an Ally

The Lost Art of Listening

Listening is a magnetic and strange thing, a creative force. The friends who listen to us are the ones we move toward. When we are listened to, it creates us, makes us unfold and expand.

Karl A. Menninger

Take a close look at the photo on this page. It happens to be Chip's youngest granddaughter, Cassie. But she could be your son, daughter, grandchild, or someone special to you. Now imagine you are in a quiet, undistracted conversation with your "Cassie." If we could secretly eavesdrop on that dialogue, what would be its features?

You would likely be noticeably gentle—softly gauging your cadence and comportment in a fashion that conveys warmth and acceptance. You would likely be completely nonjudgmental and valuing in your style, manner, and attitude. Your interest would be telegraphed through sincere eye hugs, total openness, and complete authenticity.

You would care more about cultivating inclusiveness than making an impression, more about fostering trust than winning a point. You would be intensely curious and loudly affirming no matter the elegance of what you heard.

We typically display our most ideal self when communicating with an innocent child. Stripped of pretension, agenda, and plot, we unleash a reciprocal innocence that triggers confidence and courage. The result can nurture self-esteem and bolster pride. Think of your "Cassie" the next time you are in any important conversation or any unimportant conversation with an important person. To paraphrase a well-known truism—listen to others with the best that you have and the best will come back to you.

Knowing that listening is important and *being* a good listener are two very different things. Ask employees about the listening skills of their bosses, and most will give them at best a C+. With zillions of books on how leaders should listen, why do employees continue to ding their bosses on listening? Is this a competence crisis?

In our experience, the gap between "should" and "would" has less to do with communication management than with noise management. Most leaders *can* be great listeners. Let their eight-year-old come home crying about a neighborhood conflict and you will see great listening. Zero in on a quiet corner conversation in the funeral home during the wake for a friend and you will see great listening. Put a leader between a hostile union steward and a potential shut-you-down strike and you will witness some of the best listening in history. Yet mix the normal pace of work, the typical persona of "I'm the boss," and the traditional orientation that "employees don't need to be babied," and you have the prescription for "just get to the punch line" leader listening.

Listening is crucial to mentoring. Ask fifty people who had great mentors what attribute they found most crucial, and forty-nine will probably mention their mentors' listening: "I felt I had his undivided attention when I most needed it." "You felt there was absolutely nothing happening on the face of the globe but you, her, and your problem." "He was so engaged in my concern that his secretary had to interrupt us to tell him his phone had been ringing. *I* sure wasn't going to mention it."

How do the best mentors evade the demands of daily distractions to give dedicated listening? The sounds of great listening tell us effective listeners don't *start* doing anything special—they *stop* doing something normal.

Use Raffle Listening: Focus on Focus

We have all been to a raffle! When it comes time to draw a name or ticket number, even the biggest blabbermouth present will stop verbosity to hear the verdict. Great mentors get focused and stay focused. When listening is their goal, they make it *the* priority. They do not let *anything* distract. A wise leader once said, "There are no individuals at work more important to your success than your employees—not your boss, not your customers, not your vendors. When an employee needs you to listen, pretend you just got a gift of five minutes with your greatest hero. For me, it's Abraham Lincoln." What a great concept! Think about it. If you could have five minutes—and *only* five minutes—with Moses, Mozart, or Mother Teresa, would you let a call from your boss, your customer, or *anyone* eat up part of that precious time? Treat your employees with the same focus and priority.

"Hold my calls," "Let's get out of here so we can really talk," or "Tell him I'll have to call back," are words that telegraph noise management. They say to employees, "What you have to say is so important that I don't want to miss a single word." If you cannot give employees the "I've got five minutes with Bill Gates, Oprah Winfrey, or Billy Graham" kind of focus, postpone the encounter until you can. It's better to say, "Jill, I want to give you my undivided attention. But I'm two hours from a crucial meeting and, to be perfectly honest, I would be giving you only half my attention. Can we schedule this later today when I can really focus?"

Do You Look to Your Protégé Like You Are Listening?

Try this the next time you need to listen to someone: imagine that you're a newspaper reporter from another culture sent here on assignment to get the story and report it. Your readers cannot see, hear, or feel this story except through your words. They also know nothing about the culture; you must rely on every tiny clue, nuance, and symbol to get the story right.

Your first interviewee is sitting before you, talking. It is your protégé. Now in your role as a foreign reporter, describe every subtlety in the protégé's tone, gesture, or expression. Notice especially the eyes—what have been called the "windows to the soul." Pretend you do not know this person and are hearing her speak to you for the first time. Listen for her choice of words and expressions. Is there a deeper meaning behind the sentences you hear? Is there a message that is not initially obvious in the communication?

If you ask a question or make a statement, how quick is the protégé's response? What might be implied by her silence? Is her laughter polite, muted, or hearty? If her words and tone could be a song, what style of music would it be—a country song, a rap tune, a chorale, a gospel hymn? If a great painter were to use this person's words as the inspiration for a picture, what might appear on the canvas? What color is the protégé's tone or mood?

Listening, done well, is complete and sincere absorption. Ever watch Piers Morgan on CNN or Charlie Rose on PBS? Their success as interviewers lies not in their clever questions but in their terrific listening skills. Both zip right past the interviewee's words, sentences, and paragraphs to get to the real meaning. The mission of listening is to be so tuned into the other person's message that understanding becomes a copy-and-paste function from one mind to another. Perhaps the expression "meeting of the minds" should be changed to "joining of the minds." Dramatic listening is not just a rendezvous of brains; it is a uniting, a linkage, a partnership. Like all human connections, it requires constant effort and commitment.

Listen to Learn: Be a Mirror

One of the biggest challenges of anyone with children striving to be a good parent is simply to listen without an agenda. Especially if a child is the second or third child, since the first one gave you lots of practice at saying no. Whenever a child begins to catalog his concerns, convictions, or curiosity, it is natural for a parent to feel the need to make a point, teach a lesson, correct an action, or offer some caution. But when a parent finally gives up trying to be a smart daddy and mommy and simply works at being a mirror, a child will begin to open up, trust, and—most important—feel heard.

When asked, "How would you... ?" wise parents work hard to remember to ask what they would do—*before* offering an opinion. When a child voices frustration or concern, before answering, smart parents try first to communicate through actions that the child's message has gotten through—especially when the parent's answer is likely to be different from the one the child thought he or she was going to get. The adage "You are not eligible to change my view until you first show that you understand my view" serves you in two ways. First, it helps you stay focused on being heard rather than making points. Second, it tells your listener that he is important.

Put Your Protégé in Charge of Cueing You

Being a poor listener is habit forming. Focusing takes effort; mirroring takes patience. Meanwhile, the clock is ticking on getting that order out, you are eager to check your iPhone, two calls are on hold, three people are pacing the waiting room, and you're finishing up a meeting with your protégé. Who could be a great listener under these circumstances? Answer: not even Superman! You need assistance from the only person who can help you—your protégé!

Here's how you ask for it: "George, I need your help. I know there are times when I'm not the listener I want to be. But most of the time when I'm being a lousy listener, I'm not aware I'm doing it. That's where you can help. When you think you're not getting my undivided attention, I'd appreciate your letting me know. I may get better, I may reschedule our meeting to a better time, or I may just keep on being a lousy listener. But I don't have a shot at improving unless I know when I need to, and you're the best person to tell me."

Protégés are not stupid. They will hear the words of your request, but they'll be skeptical until they see you act. You may have to ask several times before your protégé takes you at your word. And unless you express your gratitude—no matter how accurate the assessment or how successful the result—your protégé may decide not to risk your displeasure and withdraw. Prime the feedback pump, conscientiously listen to and value whatever you get, and, in time, the quality and helpfulness of the feedback will improve.

Good mentors do not listen passively; they listen dramatically. They demonstrate through their words and actions that the thoughts of their protégés are welcome and useful. When people feel heard, they feel valued. Feeling valued, they are more likely to take risks and experiment. Only through trying new steps do they grow and learn. The bottom line is this: if your goal is to be a great mentor, start by using your noise-management skills to help you fully use your talents as a great listener.

13

"Give-and-Take" Starts with "Give"
Distinguished Dialogues

"Real isn't how you are made," said the Skin Horse. "It's a thing that happens to you.... It doesn't happen all at once, you become. It takes a long time. That's why it doesn't often happen to people who break easily, or have sharp edges, or who have to be carefully kept."

Margery Williams, *The Velveteen Rabbit*

Dialogue is defined as an "interchange of ideas, especially when open and frank, as in seeking mutual understanding or harmony." Effective dialogue—with emphasis on "di," meaning "two"—requires a level playing field, equality, and give-and-take. These dynamics raise dialogue from a simple question-and-answer session to a rich, creative interaction that is more than the sum of its parts. Dialogues are distinguished when they foster becoming real.

Recall the conversations you have most valued in your life. What elements made the dialogue positive and productive? You can probably identify several. First, each player valued the view of the other, even if the views were different. The give-and-take was one in which both parties could give undivided attention and keep the dialogue focused. Finally, the outcome was that learning occurred, issues were resolved, or understanding was reached. These three components—valuing, give-and-take, and closure—will form the basis of our look at dialogue in the mentoring relationship.

The Magic of Mind-Set

There is a moment in the Edward Albee play *Who's Afraid of Virginia Woolf?* in which George and Martha (played in the film version by Richard Burton and Elizabeth Taylor) stop their perpetual oral battle to discover that they have been arguing over completely different subjects. The same thing often happens, at various decibel levels, in our own conversations. "What were we talking about?" "I forgot what I was saying," and "Where were we?" tell us that we're involved in off-track, out-of-sync, or unrelated conversations.

"Mind-set" is the term for the tone-setting actions at the beginning of a discussion that ensure a meeting of the minds on three simple but powerful questions. If both mentor and protégé are of one mind on these questions, the discussion will probably have a positive outcome.

- **Why are we here?** Both parties need to be clear on the purpose of the conversation. A simple statement followed by confirmation is usually enough: "John, I see this session as an opportunity for the two of us to discuss the best approach for conducting the Patterson study. Is that your goal as well?"

- **What will it mean to you?** The potential for both participants to benefit from the dialogue is important. Not only does it help focus the exchange, but it enhances motivation. Proper attention to the potential benefits for the protégé can turn a lethargic, "Here we go again, another meeting with Kaylee" mind-set into "Wow, this meeting with Kaylee is going to be really helpful!" The mentor derives the satisfaction of helping the protégé learn to the benefit of all.

- **How shall we talk?** Mind-set also includes telegraphing the tone and style needed. Even if the tone is implied, a brief reminder can be useful in serving notice that an open, candid, freewheeling conversation is needed and expected. It also helps clarify the rules of engagement, avoiding unpleasant surprises: "Gilbert, I'll be as open and candid as I can in this discussion. My thought was that we devote about thirty minutes to exploring options, and then give you a chance to make a decision."

Priming the Pump

The expression "priming the pump" has real meaning for people who grew up in a rural area in the fifties. Located in the most rural backyards, water pumps required priming to function. You literally "seeded" water from the ground by pouring a large pitcher of water into the top and then pumping madly up and down on the handle. To a young child who thought that on-demand water came only from a faucet, "water making"—wringing water out of the earth by your own efforts—had special magic.

If there is ever a time when the word "catalyst" applies to the role of mentor, it is during dialogue. The human version of priming the pump is assisting insight making by helping the discussion accomplish its function. There are five skills associated with catalyzing the give-and-take of dialogue: asking initiating or clarifying questions, paraphrasing, summarizing, extending, and using nonverbal cues.

Ask Initiating or Clarifying Questions

An earlier chapter, on Socrates' great secret (chapter 11), explored the art of stimulating learning by asking questions. The questions that work best are those that are direct but not leading, especially open-ended questions, those beginning with what, when, where, or how. Here are some examples of open-ended questions helpful in initiating and clarifying:

"What was the most challenging part of the task?"
"How did your team approach the problem?"

"Describe what makes this technique important."

"What are your remaining questions?"

"What have I not asked that you think would be helpful for me to know?"

Paraphrase

The purpose of paraphrasing is to demonstrate that you are listening and that you understand what is being communicated—as though holding a mirror to the discussion. Protégés appreciate knowing that they have been heard accurately, and this serves to prime the discussion pump.

There are four types of paraphrasing:

1. **Restatement.** In your own words, rather than the protégé's, state a condensed version of what the protégé said. Don't simply parrot or repeat the protégé's exact words; this communicates that you heard the protégé's statement but not that you understood it.

2. **General to specific.** If the protégé's statement is a generalization, you might paraphrase it in more specific terms by expanding on one part of the statement or by giving an example. By stating the specific, you show that you understand the general.

3. **Specific to general.** If the protégé's statement is specific, paraphrase by stating a generalization or principle. By formulating a broader response, you indicate not only that you understand the protégé's statement but also that the protégé's statement can, in fact, be generalized.

4. **Restatement in opposite terms.** Convey that you understand the meaning of the protégé's statement by restating it in opposite terms. For example, if the protégé says that a manager should do something, you can restate by saying that the manager should not do the opposite.

Consider the following statement: "Effective auditing requires the auditor to have a special kind of cautious optimism." As mentor, you might paraphrase this statement in any of the following ways:

Restatement: "You are saying that the auditor should be open but still careful."

General to specific: "An auditor should carefully check every entry."

Specific to general: "Sounds as though you think auditing is complex."

Restatement in opposite terms: "You mean that the auditor should not be negative and overly suspicious."

Paraphrasing encourages protégés to say more because they know they have been understood. An important point to remember is to look for a sign that the protégé agrees with your interpretation. If no sign is given, either verbal or nonverbal, ask the protégé whether you've paraphrased the statement accurately. If you make mistakes without checking, then you are demonstrating misunderstanding, which will fog the discussion and dampen the learning climate.

One last point on paraphrasing: notice in the examples above that each sentence ends in a period. The goal of paraphrasing is to mirror or reflect your understanding, not to ask a question or make an exclamation. Keep the focus on the protégé. Make certain your inflection turns down, not up. Asking a question puts you in control. Making a statement that ends in an exclamation point calls attention to you. Your goal is to leave the protégé in control and simply mirror what he or she is communicating.

Summarize

Summarizing is similar to paraphrasing. The difference is that the goal of paraphrasing is to *mirror the meaning* to check for understanding, whereas the goal of summarizing is to *synthesize* to check for understanding. You synthesize by condensing the meaning of the protégé's comments into a sentence or two (or, if the comments were lengthy, into a paragraph) and repeating the synthesized information as a summary.

Summarizing typically begins with such phrases as

"In other words, you believe that...,"
"What you're saying is that...," and
"In summary, you think that . . ."

Be careful about how you use certain phrases when summarizing. For example, too many uses of a catchphrase such as "What I hear you saying is..." can begin to sound mechanical and condescending.

Extend

The purpose of extending is to add scope or depth to a protégé's comments. If what you add matches the spirit of what the protégé said, it not only communicates understanding but also enriches or expands understanding. Both technical information and information about personal views and feelings can be extended.

Technical information refers to building on the factual content of the protégé's comment. An example might be, "You make a good point about the auditor's role in analyzing the corporation's financial statement. In addition, the auditor needs to ensure that all current regulations are met."

Information about personal views and feelings is what a learner says about herself during the discussion. You can add to this kind of information, but do so with care. It is a very powerful method for demonstrating deep understanding, but it is also quite difficult to do convincingly and effectively. Extending in this way requires you to empathize strongly with the protégé. Here are two examples of what a mentor might say when extending personal information:

"So you advised your colleague to sue. I was once in exactly the same position. I supervised the diversity function of human resources, and . . ."

"I agree. After I recovered from the initial shock of my father's dementia, I felt lonely and angry as well."

Use Gestures and Body Stance

Your nonverbal behavior can prime the pump of discussion and contribute to a positive learning environment by helping to communicate your understanding. Conversely, certain nonverbal behaviors can have a detrimental effect: shaking your head in disapproval, rolling your eyes to the ceiling, frowning, or suddenly moving forward in your chair. These may convey a negative judgment and make the protégé less inclined to take risks.

An appropriate gesture is to nod your head or say "uh-huh" to indicate understanding and encourage further dialogue. But don't overdo either of these cues or the protégé may feel that you are trying to manipulate the discussion rather than simply listening and encouraging.

Dos and Don'ts for Dialogues

Dialogues are interpersonal crucibles for blending facts, figures, and feelings to concoct acumen and understanding. Dialogues are most powerful when you

- listen,
- do not teach,
- allow disagreement,
- create a warm, encouraging climate,
- are aware of the learning that is taking place,
- work as hard to learn from protégés as you hope they do from you, and
- do not pressure protégés to answer or behave as you think they should.

Above all, be authentic. Just be yourself while setting the tone, asking questions, and summing up discussions with your protégé rather than doing anything artificial or manipulative to keep the give-and-take going.

Discussions are opportunities for protégés to enhance their learning, not for the mentor to teach. Stay out of the way as much as possible to let the protégé do his or her own thinking. Try not to dominate the discussion. You need not comment on everything the protégé says. Sometimes a simple "Good!" or "Thank you" is best.

Jack Gamble on Dialogues

("Mentoring in Action" Revisited)

Jack took another stab at the issue. "How does he react when you get stern and serious?"

"I'm not sure," Tracy responded.

Jack tried again. "Let me ask it this way: if I asked Adam to candidly describe you when the two of you talk about his performance, what words would he use?"

Tracy's demeanor began to change. It was as if the wheels of wisdom were turning in her head.

"He would say I was relentlessly patient." She was still half lost in thought.

"What else?"

Tracy responded with near excitement in her voice. "He would *not* describe me as tough, demanding, or disciplined."

Jack sensed that she was solving her own issue. Again, he paused before raising another question. He knew instinctively that pace was everything when insight was the goal. "So what do you think should be your next step?"

Tracy began to outline steps: a serious conversation, a performance plan, short-term goals with clear feedback, supervision with a shorter leash, and, above all, less understanding and more discipline. Jack offered a few ideas, but mostly affirmation and encouragement. They parted with an agreement to revisit the issue in a few days.

14

Simply Listen

An Interview with Deanna Mulligan,
President and CEO of the Guardian
Life Insurance Company of America

**How would you characterize or describe your most important
mentor?**

I have a number of important mentors, so it is difficult for me
to pick the most important one; however, one of my very influential mentors is calm and thoughtful, almost Zen-like. His
personality leads one to believe he is in control of nearly every
situation. I have tried to emulate his calm, fact-based emotional
detachment in certain situations.

**What were the traits you found most instrumental in your men-
tor's work with you?**

The trait of listening has been most instrumental in my mentor's work with me. No matter what is on my mind or how
urgently I want information, he calmly asks me one, possibly
two questions, and then listens to my answers. Sometimes he

comments; sometimes he doesn't. By the end of my story, I have usually solved my own problem! I reflect back on this and it seems so easy, but it's not. It is difficult to be silent, particularly when someone comes to you with a question or problem. It is so tempting to jump in and try to solve it for them. But by simply listening, you can sometimes help other people resolve their own problems.

What is one example or incident or illustration of how this person was helpful to you?

There are many examples, but I think of a time when I did something that wasn't successful. I met with my mentor and told him what had happened, that I hadn't met my goal, and I had come to the conclusion that I wasn't cut out for the particular activity and wasn't going to do it again. He listened and then said, "Are you sure?" I said, "Yes, I know I am not cut out for this." He said, "That's good thinking." It had such a big impact on me! Normally he would just listen and nod and let me figure things out for myself. If he agreed, he wouldn't say much. If he disagreed, he might say something like "Well, is that so?" In this particular case, he agreed with me. I almost panicked. "He never agrees with me," I thought. "He lets me work things out on my own." I hadn't really wanted him to tell me that I wasn't particularly suited for this activity, but he had agreed! Weighing in was rare for him, and I knew it was honest and heartfelt. So I took it to heart. The moral of the story, for me, in all three of the questions asked so far, is that it is very possible to make a big impact on someone by (1) just listening and (2) reserving judgment unless the case is really extreme. Sometimes that's all a person needs, just someone to listen. If a mentor is constantly trying to give advice, sometimes it doesn't meet its mark. But if the mentor is a listener, when they do give advice, it is really impactful.

What advice or feedback did this person provide that was helpful to you?

> The advice that has been so helpful to me is that the power of listening is enormous. I try to remember this when I mentor people. Just sitting and listening, resisting the temptation to jump in with advice or show how smart you are can be so useful to the other person. It's also okay to ask yourself, "What is my role here? What am I in this for?" I am trying to help the other person as much as possible, and clearly they just need a chance to talk an issue out. They don't necessarily want my advice. They just want to listen to themselves and they want me to listen to them. This concept has been enormously helpful to me as I mentor others. A mentor is not just someone to look up to and ask questions of; a mentor is also a sounding board as a person attempts to grow and develop in his or her profession.

GIFTING—THE MAIN EVENT

Generosity is not giving me that which I need more than you do, but it is giving me that which you need more than I do.

Khalil Gibran

Gifting is an assertive stance, not a reciprocal one. True gifting is the expression of abundance without any expectation of a gesture in response. And it is a deliberate and intentional action rather than simply a personality trait or kind manner. When gifting happens, the world moves in response.

Steve Curtin is a successful customer service consultant and a friend of ours. He tells a great story about the power of gifting. His seven-year-old's soccer team went to a frozen yogurt shop for some treats after a game. We'll let Steve tell his story.

"The first girl to receive her yogurt, Anna, sat by herself at one of the tables while the other girls waited on their yogurt orders. Anna is new to the team while the rest of the girls have played soccer together for two full seasons.

"As the other girls began receiving their yogurts, one by one they sat together at a table across from Anna's. One of the girls, after receiving her order, chose to sit with Anna. However, before she could sit down, one of her teammates pulled her chair over to the crowded table and said, 'Here, Kennedy, sit with us!'

"Instead, Kennedy slid the chair back to Anna's table and said, 'I'm going to sit with Anna.'

"And with that, one by one, every girl who was seated at the crowded table moved her chair over to Anna's table. And then they were a team."

After you extend the invitation to the mentoring process (through surrendering) and establish the relationship (through accepting), the platform is set for the main event: gifting. Essentially, the protégé is in the presence of the mentor for the gifts the mentor can offer. However, the way this encounter is managed can make a dramatic difference in the quality of both the learning and its retention.

Gifting is an expression of generosity. It is different from giving. "Giving" often implies some reciprocal toll; "gifting" is the bestowing of assets without any expectation of return. The spirit of gifting changes the nature of the relationship from guilt-based indebtedness to joy-driven partnership. And the alliance of mentor and protégé is far healthier when the pleasure of teaching exactly matches the enchantment of learning. Why is this so?

Relationships are healthier when there is some reciprocity or balance—not perfectly fifty-fifty, but some appropriate level of fairness. Most learner-takers, however, feel indebted to their mentor-givers: "She gives so much, and I have nothing to give in return." This is how guilt, liability, and obligation get started. Such anxieties, no matter how subliminal, get in the way of effective development. The learner has no tangible way to balance the relationship, at least in the short run. So it is important for the mentor to show that she has been amply rewarded by the opportunity to mentor and the pleasure inherent in the process. Reciprocity is the mentor's saying indirectly to the protégé, "My payment is the sheer joy I get from seeing you grow and learn. You owe me nothing."

The next six chapters will explore several dimensions of gifting. The opening chapter in this part zeroes in on the most frequent gift associated with mentoring: advice. The challenge mentors face is how to deliver advice without surfacing protégé resistance. The next chapter examines another important gift, that of feedback. Learner motivation is enhanced by the protégé's perceiving a valued purpose in the learning. It is incumbent on the mentor to communicate the rationale for what is to be learned. Balance is another important contribution to the learning process. Stories have been the tools of learner discovery since the campfire was invented. A section on mentor gifts would not be complete without a piece on storytelling. The last chapter addresses perhaps the most important gift of the mentor: passion. Few attitudes fuel the excitement of a learner more than to witness her or his mentor excited by the process of learning and zealous about prospects of protégé growth. In the next part, we look at this phase of mentoring from the protégé's side, a perspective that also shows how great mentors deal with the guilt and gratitude that accompany gifting.

15

Avoiding Thin Ice

The Gift of *Advice*

There is no human problem which could not be solved if people would simply do as I advise.

Gore Vidal

Someone once asked famed football coach turned ESPN commentator Lou Holtz what he considered to be the toughest part of his job as a coach. With his typical "aw shucks" charm, he finessed the question but ultimately communicated that one of the hardest parts was "teaching lessons that stay taught."

Mentors have a similar challenge. Mentoring can involve everything from chalkboard teaching to spirited discussion to circulation of relevant articles, but one of its most challenging parts is giving advice. Recall the last time someone said, "Let me give you a little advice!" No doubt it quickly put you into a defensive posture.

Psychologists remind us that we all have authority hang-ups of varying severity. So does your protégé—and the protégé's resistance to advice creates the challenge in teaching lessons that stay taught. As one frustrated supervisor commented, "I tell 'em what they ought to do, but it seems to go in one ear and out the other!"

Giving Advice Without Getting Resistance

Advice giving works only in the context of learning—that is, when you are offering advice because you believe that the protégé's performance will be improved if his knowledge or skill is enhanced. This is important, because for advice giving truly to work, you must be ready for the protégé to choose *not* to take your advice. If the protégé has no real choice about honoring your advice, then you should simply give a directive and be done with it. Couching your requirement as advice is manipulative and will only foster distrust and resentment.

There are four steps for making your advice giving more powerful and more productive. Pay attention to the sequence; it is crucial to your success.

Step 1: Clearly State the Performance Problem or Learning Goal

Begin your advice giving by letting the protégé know the focus or intent of your mentoring. Suppose you're offering advice about improving the performance of a new skill the protégé is trying to master. You might say, "George, I wanted to talk with you about the fact that although your last quarter call rate was up, your sales were down 20 percent." For advice giving to work, you must be very specific and clear in your statement. Ambiguity clouds the conversation and risks leaving the protégé more confused than enlightened.

Stating the focus—an important coaching technique in general—helps sort out the form and content of the advice. Is the problem something that is not working or something that is lacking? Stated differently, is the occasion for the advice a skill deficiency (requiring mentoring) or a will deficiency (requiring coaching)? Being clear up front about the purpose of your advice can help focus your scattergun thoughts into laser-like advice.

Step 2: Make Sure You Agree on the Focus

If what seems to you a performance challenge is seen by the protégé as something else, your advice will be viewed as overcontrolling or smothering. Make sure the protégé is as eager to improve as you are to see him improve. You may learn that the protégé has already determined what to do and has little need for your advice. Your goal is to hear the protégé say something like, "Yes, I've been concerned about that as well."

What do you do if you think there is something the protégé needs to learn but the protégé is unwilling? Many lessons get "taught" (but not learned) under this scenario. As Abraham Lincoln said, "A person convinced against his will is of the same opinion still."

Take a broader perspective. If a performance deficiency needs to be remedied, have available objective information that you both can examine. If all else fails, wait until the protégé shows more readiness to learn. To abuse the adage: you can lead a horse to water, but you can't make him think. Although protégés are by no means horses, they can sometimes be as stubborn.

Step 3: Ask Permission to Give Advice

This is the most important step. Your goal at this point is twofold: (1) to communicate advice without eliciting protégé resistance and (2) to keep ownership of the challenge with the protégé. This does not mean asking, "May I have your permission to . . .?" Rather, you might say, "I have some ideas on how you might improve if that would be helpful to you."

I know what you're thinking. What fool is going to tell her boss, "I'm not interested in your advice!"? Most protégés will heed your advice, of course, and many will be grateful for it. But remember, your goal is to communicate in a way that minimizes the protégé's being controlled or coerced—especially the *perception* of being controlled.

The essence of resistance is control. None of us is thrilled to be told what to do, and some are more defiant than others. So what do you do if, despite your best efforts, you sense protégé resistance?

Two rules: (1) Never resist resistance. Back off; take a second. Examine your stance, tone, choice of words to see whether you might be inadvertently fueling the resistance.

Then: (2) Name the issue and take the hit! Sometimes, simply stating in a low-key, nonconfrontational way how you see the situation—while assuming culpability—can drain the tension. You could say something like this: "I could be wrong on this, but I worry that I may have come on too strong just now and implied that I was commanding you. That was not my intent."

Step 4: State Your Advice in First Person Singular

Phrases like "you ought to" quickly raise resistance! By keeping your advice in the first-person singular—"what *I* found helpful" or "what worked for *me*"—helps eliminate the shoulds and ought-tos. The protégé will hear such advice unscreened by defensiveness or resistance.

A Drama in Four Steps

Now let's put the steps together in a role play to illustrate the tone and technique of advice giving. Billy is a new reservations clerk for Mayday Airlines; Kay is his section leader. Mayday has just installed a new reservation system. Some of the features are similar to the old system on which Billy was an expert. Some of the steps can be done several ways. Kay has observed that Billy follows a mass-pull-sort approach on the new system, as he did on the old. She believes Billy's efficiency would improve if he used a pull-mass-spread-sort approach.

Kay: "Billy, I've been impressed with your work. I've also noticed that your pace seems to slow when you use the mass-pull-sort approach."

Billy: "Yes, I must admit I find doing it that way a lot more comfortable. I guess using it for ten years has something to do with it."

Kay: "I know exactly what you mean. It was tough for me to let go of some of the older approaches, especially when I was evaluated on speed and shifting to a new approach would slow me down at first. I've been watching how you do it, and I have a suggestion that might help improve your speed over time."

Billy: "Shoot. I'm all ears if it helps me get faster."

Kay: "I found that the pull-mass-spread-sort approach, while awkward at first, gave me a lot more control over the reservation fields and was actually easier after a day or so than mass-pull-sort. I'll be honest with you—if someone had just told me it would be easier, I wouldn't have believed it. But I tried it and was really surprised. You might want to try it yourself."

Billy: "Sounds all right. I'll give it a try."

And they all lived happily ever after, of course.

Giving advice is like playing pinball: only by pushing and pulling can you encourage the ball to go in a new direction and increase your score. But too much pushing and pulling can cause a tilt and stop the game. Effective mentors recognize the challenge of "teaching so it stays taught" and meet that challenge by coupling their wisdom with sensitivity. They keep the ball in play as long as they can by judicious application of pushes and pulls, nudges and bumps, building the score—the protégé's competence.

Jack Gamble on Advice Giving

("Mentoring In Action" Revisited)

Jack waited to make sure she had no more to say about the subject. "How can I help?" he asked, not wanting to assume anything yet about whether his assistance was required.

Tracy looked straight at him. "I guess I need you to be a sounding board, and maybe give me some ideas on how to get him fired up—or fired."

"What do you think the problem is, based on what you know?" asked Jack.

"His morale is lousy. When I try to talk with him about his performance, his nonverbals are rather patronizing, like he's offended that I raised the issue."

Jack thought for a minute. "I can see that would be a tough nut to crack. I've never been really comfortable dealing with negative performers. It always makes me feel anxious if I have to get tough with an employee. I can see— "

"But you still manage to get them turned around," interrupted Tracy.

Jack could see that Tracy thought he had some magical secret he had kept to himself. "You believe there's a special technique that maybe you've missed."

"Yes, I suppose I do, in a way. You make it look easy. I remember when you had to terminate Edsel Joiner. The guy ended up thanking you for it!"

Jack did not respond for a while. Tracy suddenly felt awkward, as though she had allowed her stream of emotion to overflow its banks. Then, with unusual emotion in his voice, Jack said, "That was the scariest thing I've ever done since I came to work here." They both sat in silence.

16

Reporting on Blind Spots

The Gifts of *Feedback* and *Feedforward*

*Honest criticism is hard to take, particularly from a relative, a friend, an ac-
quaintance, or a stranger.*

Franklin P. Jones

Ken Blanchard is credited with labeling the word "feedback" as the
"breakfast of champions." Ken was giving us more than a clever
sound bite by borrowing from the tagline from the familiar Wheat-
ies® cereal ad. When you dissect the word into its parts—"feed"
and "back"—you get the intended connotation of feedback as a
tool for nurturing wisdom. Think of it as learning fuel. And given
that breakfast is the most important meal of the day, the symbolism
is far more significant than calling it the "supper of champions."

How do you give feedback intended to fuel growth? Start by
recognizing that, while giving advice can surface resistance, giving
feedback can stir up resentment. Advice is about expanding the
scope of knowledge; feedback is about filling a blind spot. We'll
illustrate with a true-life experience.

In the late sixties, Chip served in Vietnam as an army infantry
unit commander with the 82nd Airborne. Attached to his combat

unit was an artillery officer who worked as the forward observer (FO) for the artillery unit that supported field operations in the rear area. This FO essentially served as the eyes for the gunner pulling the lanyard on the artillery piece. As rounds were fired several miles out, the FO observed their impact and, using a field radio, called back corrections to improve the accuracy of the next artillery shot.

The FO never responded with, "Lousy shot," or, "Well, that was better than last week." He would simply say, "Drop one hundred meters," or "West one-fifty," or "Pay dirt!" This was feedback, not advice; the FO had a perspective the gunner needed and did not have.

There is one key difference between artillery feedback and mentoring feedback: artillery feedback is not likely to make the recipient angry. Advice is expertise the protégé may have or could acquire. Resistance to advice is therefore about premature smartness—that is, "You (the mentor) are telling me (the protégé) something you know that, in time, I might learn on my own." But with feedback, the issue is this: "you (the mentor) are telling me something you know that I (the protégé) will never learn on my own, and that irritates me." The danger with advice is potential resistance; with feedback, it is potential resentment.

"But what about confirming feedback?" you may be thinking. "Surely protégés won't resent feedback that communicates that their efforts are on target." To the protégé, however, such well-intentioned confirmation can seem patronizing. The unspoken reply to your "This report you wrote is complete and effective" may be "What gives you the right to tell me this?"

We have an acquaintance who is legally blind. She is in no way self-conscious about her special challenge. At a dinner party, a close friend asked her, "What is the hardest part about being blind?" She replied, "When people assist me, I sometimes cannot tell if the help is for my preservation or their pretension." Confirming feedback should contain the same level of care as corrective feedback.

Serving the Breakfast of Champions

How does a mentor bestow a gift that by its nature reminds the protégé of his or her inability to see it? Below are five steps that can make giving feedback more powerful and more productive. The steps are numbered because the order is vital to their effectiveness.

Step 1: Create a Climate of Identification—"I'm Like You"

A key factor in giving feedback is the protégé's embarrassment or awkwardness over some blind spot. Granted, embarrassment might at times be too strong a label for the protégé's feelings, but at other times it is not strong enough. In any event, the mentor can enhance the protégé's receptivity by creating a climate of identification. Make comments that have an "I'm like you"—that is, "not perfect or flawless" message. This need not be a major production—just a sentence or two to establish rapport.

Step 2: State the Rationale for the Feedback

In addition to overcoming embarrassment about the blind spot, the protégé will need to understand the context of the feedback. Help the protégé gain a clear sense of the reason or reasons the feedback is being given. Ensure that there is a clear perspective for making sense of the feedback. When you give feedback, you never want to make the protégé wonder, "Why is she telling me this?" or "How in the world can I benefit from this?"

Step 3: Assume You're Giving Yourself the Feedback

Besides being clear and empathetic, feedback must be straightforward and honest. This does not mean it must be blunt or cruel; it means that the protégé should not be left wondering, "What did she *not* tell me that I needed to hear?" Trust is born of clean communication. Think of your goal this way: how would you deliver the feedback if you were giving it to yourself? Take your cues from your own preferences; give feedback as you would receive it.

Step 4: Focus on the Future, Not on the Past

The protégé can do little about the past. Granted, there can be lessons learned through reflection and review. But the primary focus of feedback should be on providing a keen understanding that creates insight that leads to a new future application. This concept is so important to the "attitude" of feedback giving that we have included below a section by Marshall on the power and practice of what he calls "feedforward."

Step 5: Ask for What You Gave—Feedback

There is one action you can take that will both help you improve your mentoring and level the playing field in the protégé's mind: ask for feedback from the protégé. Remember this relationship is designed to be a partnership—reciprocal learning. Let the protégé know that you want the feedback process to work both ways. From time to time the forward observer attached to Chip's army infantry unit would ask the gunner for feedback on his FO technique. The gunner was given a shot at calling in a few corrections of his own, so to speak. It gave the infantry unit confidence to know that the dialogue was a two-way street.

The Power of Feedforward

Providing feedback has long been considered an essential skill for mentors. But there is a fundamental problem with all types of feedback: it focuses on the past, on what has already occurred—not on the infinite variety of opportunities that can happen in the future. As such, feedback can be limited and static, as opposed to expansive and dynamic.

Over the past several years, I have observed more than thirty thousand leaders as they participated in a fascinating experiential exercise. In the exercise, participants are each asked to play two roles. In one role, they are asked to provide feedforward —that is, to give someone else suggestions for the future and help as much as

they can. In the second role, they are asked to accept feedforward—
that is, to listen to the suggestions for the future and learn as much
as they can. The exercise typically lasts for ten to fifteen minutes,
and the average participant has six to seven dialogue sessions. In
the exercise participants are asked to:

- Pick one behavior that they would like to change. Changing
  this behavior should make a significant, positive difference in
  their lives.
- Describe this behavior to randomly selected fellow participants.
  This is done in one-on-one dialogues. It can be done quite simply, such as, "I want to be a better listener."
- Ask for feedforward—for two suggestions for the future that
  might help them achieve a positive change in their selected behavior. If participants have worked together in the past, they
  are not allowed to give ANY feedback about the past. They are
  only allowed to give ideas for the future.
- Listen attentively to the suggestions and take notes. Participants are not allowed to comment on the suggestions in any
  way. They are not allowed to critique the suggestions or even to
  make positive judgmental statements, such as, "That's a good
  idea."
- Thank the other participants for their suggestions.
- Ask the other persons what they would like to change.
- Provide feedforward—two suggestions aimed at helping the
  other person change.
- Say, "You are welcome" when thanked for the suggestions.
  The entire process of both giving and receiving feedforward
  usually takes about two minutes.
- Find another participant and keep repeating the process until
  the exercise is stopped.

When the exercise is finished, Marshall asks participants
to provide one word that best describes their reaction to this

experience. He asks them to complete the sentence "This exercise was..." The words provided are almost always extremely positive, such as "great," "energizing," "useful," or "helpful." One of the most commonly mentioned words is "fun!"

What is the last word that comes to mind when we consider any feedback activity? Fun!

Eleven Reasons to Try FeedForward

Participants are then asked why this exercise is seen as fun and helpful as opposed to painful, embarrassing, or uncomfortable. Their answers provide a great explanation of why feedforward can often be more useful than feedback as a developmental tool.

1. We can change the future. We can't change the past. Feedforward helps protégés envision and focus on a positive future, not a failed past. Athletes are often trained using feedforward. Race-car drivers are taught to "look at the road ahead, not at the wall." Basketball players are taught to envision the ball going in the hoop and to imagine the perfect shot. By giving protégés ideas on how they can be even more successful (as opposed to visualizing a failed past), we can increase their chances of achieving this success in the future.

2. It can be more productive to help people learn to be "right" than to prove they were "wrong." Negative feedback often becomes an exercise in "let me prove you were wrong." This tends to produce defensiveness on the part of the receiver and discomfort on the part of the sender. Even constructively delivered feedback is often seen as negative as it necessarily involves a discussion of mistakes, shortfalls, and problems. Feedforward, on the other hand, is almost always seen as positive because it focuses on solutions—not problems.

3. Feedforward is especially suited to successful people. Successful people like getting ideas that are aimed at helping them achieve

their goals. They tend to resist negative judgment. We all tend to accept feedback that is consistent with the way we see ourselves. We also tend to reject or deny feedback that is inconsistent with the way we see ourselves. Successful people tend to have a very positive self-image. Marshall has observed many successful executives respond to (and even enjoy) feedforward.

4. Feedforward can come from anyone who knows about the task. It does not require personal experience with the individual. One very common positive reaction to the previously described exercise is that participants are amazed by how much they can learn from people that they don't know! For example, if you want to be a better listener, almost any fellow leader can give you ideas on how you can improve. They don't have to know you. Feedback requires knowing about the person. Feedforward just requires having good ideas for achieving the task.

5. People do not take feedforward as personally as feedback. In theory, constructive feedback is supposed to "focus on the performance, not the person." In practice, almost all feedback is taken personally (no matter how it is delivered). Successful people's sense of identity is highly connected with their work. The more successful people are, the more this tends to be true. It is hard to give a dedicated professional feedback that is not taken personally. Feedforward cannot involve a personal critique, since it is discussing something that has not yet happened! Positive suggestions tend to be seen as objective advice—personal critiques are often viewed as personal attacks.

6. Feedback can reinforce personal stereotyping and negative self-fulfilling prophecies. Feedforward can reinforce the possibility of change. Feedback can reinforce the feeling of failure. How many of us have been "helped" by a spouse, significant other, or friend, who seems to have a near-photographic memory of our previous "sins" that they share with us in order to point out the history of our shortcomings. Negative feedback can be used to reinforce the message "this is just the way you are."

Feedforward is based on the assumption that the receiver of suggestions can make positive changes in the future.

7. Face it! Most of us hate getting negative feedback, and we don't like to give it. I have reviewed summary 360-degree feedback reports for over fifty companies. The items "provides developmental feedback in a timely manner" and "encourages and accepts constructive criticism" both always score near the bottom on coworker satisfaction with leaders. Traditional training does not seem to make a great deal of difference. If leaders got better at providing feedback every time the performance appraisal forms were "improved," most should be perfect by now! Leaders are not very good at giving or receiving negative feedback. It is unlikely that this will change in the near future.

8. Feedforward can cover almost all of the same "material" as feedback. Imagine that you have just made a terrible presentation in front of the executive committee. Your mentor is in the room. Rather than make you "relive" this humiliating experience, your mentor might help you prepare for future presentations by giving you suggestions for the future. These suggestions can be very specific and still delivered in a positive way. In this way your mentor can "cover the same points" without feeling embarrassed and without making you feel even more humiliated. Your protégé can benefit from the same approach.

9. Feedforward tends to be much faster and more efficient than feedback. An excellent technique for giving ideas is to say, "Here are four ideas for the future. Please accept these in the positive spirit that they are given. If you can only use two of these ideas, you are still two ahead. Just ignore what doesn't make sense for you." With this approach, almost no time gets wasted on judging the quality of the ideas or "proving that the ideas are wrong." This "debate" time is usually negative; it can take up a lot of time, and it is often not very productive. By eliminating judgment of the ideas, you make the process much more positive for you, the mentor, as well as for your protégé. Successful

people tend to have a high need for self-determination and will tend to accept ideas that they "buy" while rejecting ideas that feel "forced" upon them.

10. Feedforward can be a useful tool to apply with anyone. Rightly or wrongly, feedback is associated with judgment. This can lead to very negative—or even career-limiting—unintended consequences. Feedforward does not imply superiority of judgment. It is more focused on being a helpful "fellow traveler" than an "expert." As such it can be easier to hear from a person who is coming from a position of power or authority.

11. Participants tend to listen more attentively to feedforward than feedback. One of Marshall's participants in the feedforward exercise noted, "I think that I listened more effectively in this exercise than I ever do at work!" When asked why, he responded, "Normally, when others are speaking, I am so busy composing a reply that will make sure that I sound smart that I am not fully listening to what the other person is saying. I am just composing my response. In feedforward the only reply that I am allowed to make is 'thank you.' Since I don't have to worry about composing a clever reply, I can focus all of my energy on listening to the other person!"

The intent of this section is to show how feedforward can often be preferable to feedback in day-to-day interactions. Aside from its effectiveness and efficiency, feedforward can make life a lot more enjoyable. When managers are asked, "How did you feel the last time you received feedback?" their most common responses are very negative. When managers are asked how they felt after receiving feedforward, they reply that feedforward was not only useful, it was also fun! Quality communication—between and among people at all levels and every department and division—is the glue that holds organizations together. By using feedforward—and by encouraging others to use it—leaders can dramatically improve the quality of communication in their organizations, ensuring that the right message is conveyed, and that those who receive it are receptive to its content. The result is a much more dynamic, much more open organization—one whose employees focus on the promise of the future rather than dwelling on the mistakes of the past.

17

Linking Proficiency to Purpose
The Gift of *Focus*

Shared vision is vital for the learning organization because it provides focus and energy for learning. Innovative learning occurs only when people are striving to accomplish something that matters deeply to them.

Peter Senge

Adult learning and child learning are different when it comes to focus. Children are patient with delayed application and the promise that "someday you'll find this helpful." Adults question the worth of knowing the correct answer to the test question about the ingredients of the pie at the king's banquet in *Beowolf*. As adults, we want real-time relevance and immediate application. And if the tie to usefulness is unclear or absent, our motivation drops and our attention drifts.

Proper protégé motivation is vital to protégé learning. Motivation is surfaced in part by linking what is being learned with a grander purpose. Call it "competence with a cause," to suggest that as learners we need the "why" as much as we need the "how." We want our pursuit to be in the direction of some desirable end point.

Focusing on Purpose

The Ritz-Carlton Hotel Company is known for extraordinary elegance and world-class customer service. Winner of two Malcolm Baldrige National Quality Awards, it achieved distinction not just through great quality but consistently great quality—across all eighty-plus hotels in over twenty-five countries. A key part of the Ritz-Carlton consistency comes through a clear vision: "We are ladies and gentlemen serving ladies and gentlemen." Every employee from property general manager to housekeeper is clear on that vision as well as its specific implications for their role.

As clear and powerful as their vision is—and the twenty customer-service practices that accompany it—it is useless unless it is kept alive and fresh. It becomes no more than a clever billfold-sized, trifold, laminated card unless it serves as the grounding and touchstone for every action and all decisions. When Ritz-Carlton employees do "line-up"—a ten-minute stand-up meeting in every department at every shift change—it includes an articulation of "what we learned today that would impact our guests' experience tomorrow." Learning is tied to purpose. Every new employee orientation begins with the vision and values, not with policies and procedures.

Nordstrom is another company that uses its employee empowerment policy—"Use your good judgment in all situations"—as the basis for many of their learning programs. "Learning at Nordstrom," says one department manager at their flagship store in downtown Seattle, "is all aimed at helping associates think like owners. Good judgment comes from good know-how." Springfield ReManufacturing goes a step further. Employees are taught business literacy skills. "We want our employees to know the skills needed to run their jobs just like it was their own business. If they don't know the impact of their everyday decisions on the profitability of the business, how can we expect them to not be wasteful or inefficient?" says CEO Jack Stack.[1]

"Why" before "What" and "How"

Mentoring with focus means taking time to help link emerging acumen with an exciting aim. It might not be the global vision of the corporation, like the forward-thinking Ritz-Carlton, but rather some short-term objective of the unit. Adult-learning guru Fredric Margolis says, "When giving learning direction, always let the 'why' come before the 'what' or the 'how.'" The crux of Margolis's point is that learners can psychologically and emotionally hear the "what" or "how" in a fundamentally different way if it is preceded by the rationale.

The rationale is always stated from the protégé's perspective, not the mentor's, or the unit's, or the organization's. Here is the difference:

From the Organization's Perspective: "When interviewing someone for a job, you may or may not choose to reveal certain things about yourself or the organization. At Acme, we believe you should know in advance what you will reveal before you begin an interview. In a moment I will provide you an opportunity to practice revealing information."

From the Protégé's Perspective: "When interviewing someone for a job, you may or may not choose to reveal certain things about yourself or the organization. What is important is that you feel comfortable and competent in revealing certain information to the person being interviewed. This feeling comes with experience. The more we risk, the better we become at taking risks. In a moment you will have the opportunity to practice revealing information."

The rationale should communicate a personal reason for learning as well as a professional reason. The reason presented should be one with which the protégé can identify, one that makes logical as well as emotional sense. It should not be a justification by the mentor in terms of the needs of the unit or the organization.

Grounding Summaries with Substance

Grounding is all about creating a foundation for learning. Grounding lends a bolstering sturdiness to new skills or knowledge. Think of the learning rationale as providing not only direction but roots as well. Building a foundation is by definition an initial act. However, foundations only support when they are maintained. An effective mentor will frequently circle back to the rationale and "help the protégé touch the touchstone." One way to do this is with a summary statement, such as "Overall, this skill is vital to what we are working to accomplish because..." Or you reinforce the foundation with a question: "Tell me again the reason this learning is important."

Adult learners need a sense of purpose to engage their enthusiasm. They need confidence to weather the storm of uncertainty and apprehension of embracing newness and change. As author Louisa May Alcott wrote, "I'm not afraid of storms, for I'm learning to sail my ship." Wise mentors can bolster purposeful learning by using vision, objectives, and rationale to ensure growth has both direction (focus) and grounding (foundation). It is not the words we speak—it is the strategy employed to elevate learning from simply a task to be accomplished to part of a grander cause and a nobler endeavor.

18

The Bluebirds' Secret
The Gift of *Balance*

Well-timed silence hath more eloquence than speech.

M. F. Tupper

This chapter was written by Chip Bell.

There's a bluebird house on an oak tree six feet from my bedroom window. The same pair of bluebirds comes each spring to build, populate, and empty a nest in it. This past spring, their parenting process caused me to reflect on how instructive bluebird flying lessons could be for mentors. Bluebirds don't just hatch eggs and depart. They act as mentors in getting a young bird from the security of the birdhouse to the serenity of flight.

Effective mentoring is especially crucial in this era of rapid change and increasing organizational complexity. Employees who don't continue to grow will be unable to cope, adapt, and succeed. Those who wait for the next opening in a much-needed training class may be quickly left behind. In times like these, the mentor becomes a key source for real-time employee learning. But combining an in-charge role with an "in-sight" goal calls for balance—and that's where the bluebirds come in.

Finding the Teachable Moment

How does the bluebird know when its fast-growing offspring is ready to be pushed from the nest? Bluebirds have genetically coded weaning instincts and an innate sense of timing. They watch for certain subtle signs of maturity: restlessness, wing strength, the eagerness of the infant's lunge toward the birdhouse exit even when there's no worm dangling from mama's beak, and a whole bunch of other stuff they haven't told the bird researchers.

One key to their attentiveness is the way they take different viewpoints. Bluebird parents often perch some distance away and call out to the baby bluebird, as though to gauge reaction time—how fast does Junior respond to the chirp? A parent bluebird might perch atop the birdhouse and peer down through the entrance hole. While it would obviously be easier to observe from inside, the bluebird knows that to get a true picture, it must balance the comfortable and familiar close-up examination with views from more dangerous and diverse angles and conditions.

Baby bluebirds and protégés need teachable moments. One of the chief complaints protégés make about their mentors is, "He was not on hand when I really needed him." This key, often brief opportunity is sometimes called "the teachable moment." The timing of this moment is important: it's a combination of the learner's readiness to learn, the quickness with which learning can be applied, and the special conditions likely to foster or support learning.

So what should a mentor do to match teaching with timing? And how does the mentor demonstrate the right amount of attention? Too much attention can leave the protégé feeling smothered; too little can make her feel abandoned.

- Stay vigilant for every opportunity to foster discovery. Whenever you communicate with the protégé, ask yourself, "Is there learning that can be derived from this?"

- Keep a lookout for signs of protégé apathy, boredom, or dullness, any of which may indicate a plateau in learning.

- Ask A and listen for B. For example, ask the question, "How would you describe the challenge in your job?" but listen for the answer as if you had asked, "How would you describe your growth or learning deficit in your job?" It is far easier for protégés to talk about being challenged or not being challenged than to discuss a learning deficit.

- From a distance, watch the protégé at work. As you watch your birdhouse from a distant railing, keep in mind that your goal is to determine whether it might be a good time to intervene as a mentor.

Support Without Rescuing

The morning the baby bluebird took that first clumsy flight from the birdhouse to the nearest bush, both parents were on hand for the occasion, proud and no doubt anxious. As the wobbly fledgling took a short, awkward burst of flight, one parent was in the tree nearby, providing comforting chirps of encouragement.

Suddenly, the family black cat Taco (Bell) came around the corner. Instantly, one of the parents flew within a few feet of Taco, distracting her long enough for the young bird to reach a limb safely out of reach. It was a beautiful display of courageous selflessness by the parent, vital and well-timed support—but the student pilot was still left to do his own flying.

Mentors provide support and encouragement as protégés work to transform shaky new skills into confident mastery. The challenges for all mentors are "When does too much support become rescuing?" and "When does too little support become a sign of callousness?" Most mentors are tempted to take help to the level of interference. Too often we say, "Let me just show you how to do

Mentor Scale and Balance

The Mentor Scale can be helpful in examining the issue of balance. Below are a few cautions based on your score on the Mentor Scale.

Sociability

Low: You may have a propensity to leave the protégé feeling abandoned. Provide more attention. Don't be so quick to mentor and run. Demonstrate your interest in and concern for your protégé.

High: You may have a tendency to smother the protégé by overassisting. Remember that too much help can be as great a liability as too little. Back off a bit and give the protégé a wonderful opportunity: the chance to fail, and thus to learn.

Dominance

Low: You may leave the protégé feeling *betrayed*. When he gets no guidance at all, the protégé can feel alone and anxious—especially early in the relationship. Let self-direction happen, but don't abdicate. Hang in there with the learner until you conclude he has wings strong enough to fly on his own.

that!" when we should be asking, "What do you think you should do next?"

The following assemble-it-yourself statement may help you find the right balance between helpful support and unhelpful rescue:

If I were really honest with myself, I would say I tend to offer help because

- I don't want to see the protégé repeat mistakes I've made.
- I can't afford too many errors in the name of learning.
- I don't want to see the protégé hurt, embarrassed, disappointed, or discouraged.
- I need to show the protégé how competent I am.
- If I don't show the protégé how, he'll never learn or become competent.

High: You may have an inclination to *rescue*. Remember that growth comes through discovery and insight. Too much control can deprive the learner of the opportunity to find them on his own. Let go of the reins and give your protégé a bit more slack.

Openness

Low: You may cause the protégé to feel *anxious*, particularly early in the relationship. Guarded behavior begets guarded behavior. Remember, your timidity, caution, and reserve will only amplify similar feelings in the protégé. Take interpersonal risks, lighten up, and communicate your feelings. It will help break the ice and relax your protégé.

High: When you are too open too soon, you can make the protégé feel apprehensive. You set a standard that learners may think they are incapable of or unwilling to model and match. Openness and vulnerability are positive attributes in a mentoring relationship. However, too much too soon can be overwhelming.

If there is one lesson the bluebirds can offer, it is the living illustration of the teacher's courage to let the learner fail. Mentors, like parents, want learning to be painless, but most significant growth happens through the discomfort of grappling for skill. En route to walking and running, knees get skinned. The bluebird dived courageously at the menacing cat as the student pilot fluttered awkwardly down the backyard runway. The parent seemed to be protecting its youngster—and more: demonstrating bravery for it. Learners dare to risk when they see the teacher take risks.

Avoid Perfection

There is one point this book makes over and over: the greatest gift a mentor can give a protégé is to demonstrate authenticity and realness. Conversely, the highest barrier to learning is an environment laced with expectations of perfection and implications of "Why can't you be as good as I am?" There's nothing wrong with mentors showing off to protégés, as long as what they are showing is their genuineness—clay feet and all. Consider the following suggestions:

- Tape your mentoring sessions to see if they contain controlling language: "I want you to...," "You should...," or the patronizing royal "we," as in "Now we must take our medicine."

- Listen for whether you are taking as many interpersonal risks as the protégé in being real and open. Do you sound like an expert or a fellow learner? Would the protégé hear you as a schoolmarm or as an experienced colleague?

- Eliminate anything that may communicate power or distance. Mentoring from behind a desk can be far more intimidating than sitting at a forty-five-degree angle without barriers. Role or position power can be an obstacle when learning is the objective. Take steps to literally and symbolically minimize its effect.

- Be open to alternative views and unique interpretations. The path to excellence zigs and zags between extreme views. Help the protégé refine her view by honoring the extreme, while asking questions to encourage the discovery of a balanced, more effective position.

- Take the learning seriously, but not yourself. Laugh *with* your protégé, never at his or her mistakes. An occasional "I made that same mistake" can melt learner apprehension and promote the risk taking needed to learn.

Our bluebirds are empty-nesters at the moment. Their fledgling has no doubt joined the world of adult bluebirds and is out hunting tasty bugs, dodging curious cats, and perhaps serving as the flight instructor for a newer generation. Like the bluebirds, the final gift of the mentor is to allow the protégé the freedom to find his or her own way.

19

Inviting Your Protégé to Enchantment

The Gift of *Story*

Storytelling reveals meaning without committing the error of defining it.

Hannah Arendt

"People are different. They don't all see things the same way." It was the opening line of a mentor's effort to help his protégé cope with the challenges of learning about relationships. The mentor continued: "It reminds me of the comic strip *Mutt and Jeff*." In the early 1960s the comic strip was one of everybody's favorites.

"Mutt and Jeff were playing a competitive game of golf and having a great time," the mentor began. "As they approached the ninth tee, they were even. As Mutt was setting up to tee off, he turns and says to Jeff, 'You know, Jeff, if everybody saw like I did, everybody would want my wife.' Jeff saw this as the perfect time to bring his starstruck buddy back to reality. 'I don't know about that, Mutt,' Jeff says. 'If everybody saw like I did, *nobody* would want your wife.' They both have a great laugh!" The corny story helped the protégé gain new insights into how important it was to try to see things through the eyes of another.

People love stories. They love to tell them and they love to hear them. A really good story makes a campfire worth lighting, a cocktail party worth attending, and a reunion worth holding. A story can evoke tears and laughter. A good story can touch something familiar in each of us and yet show us something new about our lives, our world, ourselves.

Stories can also be powerful tools for mentoring. In the words of author Rudyard Kipling, "If history were taught in the form of stories, it would never be forgotten." Stories can reach resistant protégés in ways that well-crafted advice may not. Unlike straightforward advice or feedback, stories have a way of circumventing the mind's logic to capture the imagination. As such, they are great gifts when delivered with care, content, and caution.

Most stories are either crafted or chosen. The crafted ones are "baked from scratch"; the chosen ones are "re-crafted"—in other words, tailored to fit the mentor, the protégé, and the learning objective. The objective is paramount. Stories without purpose obviously lack relevance, but they also tend to lack charm.

Setting the Stage for the World of Enchantment

Psychologist Adam Smith in his book *Powers of Mind* uses a story as a clever metaphor to illustrate the way socialization encodes us to see (and not see) certain things as we mature.[1] He quotes philosopher Aldous Huxley, who described our minds as a reducing valve, filtering out certain realities in order to prevent us from being overwhelmed with too much data.[2] Smith's story goes like this:

A small child turns to his mother and exclaims, "Look, mommy, it's a purple cow!" His wise mother gently tells the child there is no such thing as a purple cow. On another sighting the child makes a similar excited report only to receive a similar rational correction. Soon the boy quits reporting purple cows and ultimately quits seeing purple cows altogether. One might surmise the same would be true for fairies, leprechauns, gnomes, goblins, and ghosts. They might be there, but it is a reality we have all agreed we cannot see.

It is this "maybe there is another world we don't see" sentiment that forms the basis of all fairyland stories. Somewhere deep in us all is the hope that there might be more than our too often plain-vanilla world. When that hope is combined with trust (or faith in the religious sense), it can sometimes transport us to a magical world. Once there, we witness and experience enchantment. And, upon return to our everyday life, we are forever changed by our captivating trip. Once Wendy Darling and her brothers John and Michael returned with Peter Pan after visiting Neverland, the three would never be the same again. The same was true for Alice and Cinderella and Thumbelina.

The world of learning can be a magical place. When protégés open the treasure box of learning and all the joy and excitement inside spills out, they are never able to return it to the box. It becomes a part of their DNA and becomes self-directed, only needing a mentor as an escort cheering their progress, not an elbow nudging them along.

Whether a mentor chooses to craft or re-craft a story, like our opening *Mutt and Jeff* example, several key steps are involved. The first step is to clarify a story's purpose. Here's a checklist of questions to ask yourself:

- What key learning points do I hope to convey with a story?

- By using a story, am I indulging in irrelevant fantasy? Is the point best communicated by analogy?

- Is my protégé likely to appreciate the point if it's conveyed by a story? Or is he or she likely to be literal-minded and view stories as "much ado about nothing"?

- How do I convey the story so it comes alive and achieves its purpose?

Most mentors can learn to tell stories well, but some may find storytelling so challenging that they prefer to use other approaches. If you decide to incorporate a story into your mentoring discussions, you may find it helpful to structure your story around the following elements: the context, the challenge, and the climax.

The Context: Painting the Background

The story's context establishes the setting or scene. It's the "once upon a time" part that invites the protégé into the story. In a sense, the context allows the protégé to become a witness to the visions of the storyteller.

A story should start with a transition that uses words or cues—such as a long pause—to signify that a story is beginning. Protégés shouldn't wonder why you are telling them what you're telling them, and they shouldn't be asking themselves, "Where does this fit in?" The mentor in the opening paragraph prefaced his instructive story on relationships with, "People are different. They don't all see things the same way. It reminds me of the comic strip *Mutt and Jeff*."

After the transition, it's important to create a realistic backdrop. Often, a story takes more time to relate than it takes to happen, so you should allow enough time to set the scene. Our mentor's story had a setting that communicated the tone of the story: "Mutt and Jeff were playing a game of golf and having a great time. All of a sudden Mutt said to Jeff, 'You know, Jeff, if everybody saw like I did, everybody would want my wife.'"

Even well-told stories often violate grammatical rules. They commonly shift between the past tense and the present. The past tense tells what happened; the present tense is acted out.

When creating the context of your story, ask yourself the following questions:

- What do I want the protégé to feel?
- How can I build a sense of adventure, mystery, suspense, joy, or invitation?

- Will my protégé be able to visualize the scene I have in my mind?

- Will my protégé be able to identify with or relate to the story and the picture I've planned?

The Challenge: Creating the Proper Tension

A good story should contain a challenge, which can also be described as "dissonance." To communicate dissonance, it's important to create a dilemma that the protégé can identify with. Even the storytelling mentor's story had a bit of tension when he said, "Jeff saw this as the perfect time to bring his starstruck buddy back to reality."

Once you've created a dilemma, you should describe in your story plan the challenge for each of the key characters, using one sentence—for example, "John's challenge is such-and-such. Sue's challenge is such-and-such." This can help you keep things straight or "manage" the story.

The following questions can help you create dissonance:

- What do I want the protégé to feel?

- How can I build a sense of concern, conflict, or suspense?

- Will the protégé be able to visualize the challenge or challenges the same way that I do?

- Will the dilemma create enough dissonance so that the protégé will desire a resolution?

The Climax: Insight through Resolution

The story's climax is essentially a punch line with a lesson. Of course, the lesson is usually longer than the typical punch line of a joke.

The climax is more than just an ending. It's a resolution that can be used as a tool for helping the protégé to learn. The storyteller instructs through resolution, and the protégé allows his or her need for resolution to lead to the learning. The climax must clearly fit the challenge and also carry the protégé in new and somewhat unexpected directions.

If a story were mapped out, the climax would reside on the other side of the gaps created by the challenge. It the listener leaps over the gaps, thus eliminating the dissonance, he or she experiences insight and learning. But the climax must be truly inviting, realistic, and relevant. If the climax or resolution is too routine or far-fetched, there is no insight. The protégé must be able to relate to and identify with how the story ends.

When creating the climax, ask yourself the following questions:

- Will the story's ending result in learning and achieve a mentoring goal? Is a story the best way to accomplish that with this protégé?

- Will the ending surprise, amuse, challenge, or amaze?

- Will the protégé view the ending as realistic and relevant?

- Will the protégé be able to envision several possible endings before the climax is revealed?

- Will the protégé gain insight and develop new attitudes, understanding, or skills from the resolution?

At the story's end, your protégé should say, "I wouldn't have thought of that" or "I wasn't expecting that." He or she should also feel, upon reflection, that the story makes perfect sense.

Putting the Right Spin on the Tale

Even a well-crafted story can fail to achieve its objectives if it isn't told well. Here are a few techniques and tips for effectively delivering a story.

Dramatize. Don't be afraid to ham it up a bit. Remember: you're trying to paint a picture. As you speak, focus on the scene in your mind and try to become part of it. Relive the story as you tell it.

Describe. Use a lot of details in the beginning of the story and then phase them out. Listeners need to hear more details while you're creating the context. A good rule of thumb is to start by using more details than you think the story needs. Your goal is to draw your listener into the scene. Once you establish the context and you move on to the challenge and climax, you need fewer details.

Shift. As you're telling the story, you sometimes act as a guide. Other times, you're part of the action. In other words, you step in and out of the scene. These dual functions make it acceptable for the storyteller to shift between the past tense and the present tense.

Pause. Timing is key to good storytelling. So-called pregnant pauses can entice your protégé and imbue a story with drama and suspense. If you are not accustomed to telling stories, practice by recording your story on audiotape and listening for places where pauses might add punch. Then tell your story at a pace that is slow, but not too slow.

Gesture. Use different gestures, varied facial expressions, and dramatic body movements. Such techniques can help turn a written story into a living demonstration.

Stay focused. The proverbial admonition to "stick to the story" is good advice. The storyteller who goes off on tangents loses momentum and ultimately frustrates listeners. Don't introduce secondary issues or new words and concepts. And don't ask questions during the story. Questions can be effective learning tools, but they tend to break the thread of the narrative.

Stay positive. Even sad stories should have an element of joy. Avoid biting sarcasm and satire. If a story is too acerbic, protégés tend to resist. The same goes for exaggeration. Most storytellers tend to embellish stories and tailor them to fit their needs and goals. That's expected, but too much poetic license can actually undermine the authenticity and realism that make a story powerful. If your protégé does not buy your story, she or he probably won't buy your learning points either.

Stories fit just about anywhere. As an introduction, a story can announce and organize the main points of the learning to follow. As a conclusion, a story can reiterate the core principles, ideas, and concepts of the mentoring session. Stories can act as breathers. They can provide welcome respites when topics are complex or abstract, and they can alleviate emotionally charged discussions. Stories can engage learning emotionally and show protégés the consequences of taking or omitting certain actions. But it isn't enough simply to "make up a story." As with most worthwhile endeavors, effective storytelling requires thorough planning.

20

Grace Under Fire

An Interview with Joe Almeida, Chairman of the Board, President, and CEO of Covidien, plc

How would you characterize or describe your most important mentor?

My most important mentor was not a high-level, senior company executive. He was the third boss I had in my life. He was a vice president of operations for a company that I joined seventeen years ago. He had all the characteristics of a person who has gravitas. He had grace under fire. He was a calm person, and he had a drive for results. He led by example. He had an incredible ability to understand and acquire talent, and he was a very kind person.

A Marine platoon commander in the Vietnam War, my mentor had spent time on the front lines. His sergeant and soldiers depended upon his leadership. He'd seen many people die, and much human tragedy, so he understood what was important in life. Sometimes people are skewed about what is important and overreact to insignificant things. He showed me that sometimes you've got to make hard decisions under fire, so it's best to make them with a clear, calm mind. This way, the outcome is more predictable.

What were the traits you found most instrumental in your mentor's work with you?

My mentor taught me to do exactly what I just described. When I started my career, I was a hyper type of person. I over-reacted to many things that were not tremendously important or significant. Grace under fire was a great, great trait for me to learn. My mentor was very humble, which I was not. I learned from him how to leave my ego at the door every day when I came to work. And, finally, he was a great listener. He listened with intensity. He actively listened. I learned this from him.

What is one example or incident or illustration of how this person was helpful to you?

Some time ago, I received very bad news about a product we were making. We're in medical technology, and there were three deaths associated with one of our products. This rattles any senior executive who makes products designed to save people's lives. Sometimes the products are designed and produced right, but sometimes there are unintended consequences that can't be predicted. I was told what had happened by telephone on a Friday night after work. My usual tendency would have been to come up with solutions on the spot, have twenty things going on at the same time, and have everyone scramble to get things done and get back to me. But instead, I hung up the phone, called a group of four very senior executives, and very calmly told them what had happened. In thinking about what my mentor would have done, I told the group that we were going to come under fire, that there were going to be consequences, and that we need-ed to act quickly. I told them that we needed to take a little time and think about how we were going to face the crisis. We had a resolution in less than twenty-four hours. Not only that, but we were able to speak with the FDA and handle the situation in the right way, with patient safety as the top priority. If I had taken charge in my natural, hyper state, without thinking it through and without using the example of grace under fire that I had learned from Mike, the outcome would not have been good.

What advice or feedback did this person provide that was helpful to you?

My mentor told me a story about being calm. He didn't usually speak about the war, but one time he gave me an example of what he was trying to teach me. He told me that he had been down in the trenches, taking a break before going back out to fight. He said there was another soldier in the trench who was fighting the rats instead of resting. My mentor said to the soldier, "What is most important to you? To fight the rats and tell the enemy where we are, or to live to fight another day?" It took me a while to understand what he was trying to teach me with this story. But now I understand that he meant to sort out your priorities, not only in business, but in life. Ask yourself, what really makes a difference? Understand the long-term consequences of the things that you do. They may seem very small in themselves, but they are great in terms of future impact.

PART 5

EXTENDING—NURTURING A SELF-DIRECTED LEARNER

There are limits to dialogue. This book thus far has assumed that all mentoring occurs in a high-quality conversation between a mentor and a protégé. While it is true that the mentoring process is largely a conversational proceeding, it would be shortsighted and limiting to assume that dialogue is the only path to discovery and insight.

In fact, dialogue itself can be seductive, and the relationship can be codependent. Mentor and protégé in time become very comfortable with each other. The mentor derives personal satisfaction from watching the protégé learn; this leads to more conversation, more encounters. The protégé also finds pleasure in the wisdom of the mentor and the spirit of the consultation. While comfort is clearly helpful for communication, it can be a barrier to experimentation. Both mentor and protégé look forward to the next meeting, ultimately becoming so dependent on the relationship that neither is inclined to risk losing it.

While "codependent" might seem too strong a word, even a small degree of dependency can spoil the spirit of growth. The litmus test is the emotional discomfort either party would experience if the relationship came to an end. If either party's need to end the relationship is marked by guilt or resistance, some codependency has probably infiltrated the relationship.

An effective way to avoid codependency is to extend the learning beyond dialogue. As new forms of learning become available, the protégé discovers new routes to self-sufficiency. The ultimate extension takes the mentor completely out of the equation, leaving the protégé to find his or her own way to competence—and independence.

The bias of most managers is to narrow, not extend, to build loyalty rather than liberty. Consequently, this final core competence is rather counterintuitive, much like surrendering, accepting, and gifting. However, as uncomfortable as it may be, the greatest contribution you can make to the protégé's development is to let the relationship evolve to a point at which you are no longer needed. That contribution begins with extending.

Beyond the Relationship
Ensuring the Transfer of Learning

Learn as though you would never be able to master it; hold it as though you would be in fear of losing it.

Confucius (sixth century BC)

There are many advantages to being raised on a farm. You learn a lot about how nature really works. Instead of watching milk come pouring out of a carton, you get to see it come squirting out of a cow.

Before high-tech milking machines, milk made its way to your glass the long way around. It was the product of the bribery of a bag of feed, special squeezes on a reluctant udder, numerous restarts after the milk pail was kicked over or a tail in pursuit of a fly was deposited inside, slow straining through cheesecloth, plus careful skimming and cooling. All the pictures in some citified textbook could not adequately tell the tale of milk making like a seat on a three-legged stool in a smelly barn with an impatient cow.

Mentoring can be an exhilarating but ineffective experience if mentors talk like a textbook and fail to offer a seat on the stool. Mentoring does not end with advice, feedback, and instruction. The goal of mentoring is not simply learning. The goal of mentoring is to foster betterment... better performance, greater productivity, higher effectiveness. Granted, there is merit in learning for learning's sake. But in today's business world with its razor-thin margins, learning must be for result's sake. Mentors don't have the luxury of helping protégés increase their knowledge but not their use of that knowledge.

Transfer of learning has been the challenge for all learning facilitators—be they teachers, professors, trainers, or mentors. The argument often posited is "Once they leave my tutelage, it is up to them to put it to use." Great mentors know, however, that the experiment isn't over until the learner has tried it out in the laboratory of life. And there are all sorts of actions that help ensure that what is learned in the relationship actually "takes."

Lend a Helping Hand

The key word is "fellowship"—a word that combines the constitution of a partnership with the warmth of camaraderie. Look for ways to "be there" when your protégé has "opening night." Remember that rehearsal is always a far cry from the reality of actual performance. Boldness within the cloistered safety of a mentoring relationship is quite different from bravery in the school of hard knocks. When your protégé is slated to engage in her or his first attempt at "flying solo," send your good wishes and affirmation. Call after the fact to learn of the outcome. Regardless of the success or failure of the first time out, be supportive. Offer your help; do not automatically give your help. Your protégé needs to feel independent, not still saddled with a "Father knows best" Monday-morning quarterback.

If you can actually be there, assume the role of fan and cheerleader, not sideline coach. Let your protégé know you are there, feeling excited and confident. But avoid the grandstanding of the doting parent eagerly letting everyone in the stands know, "That's my kid!"

Run appropriate interference to help ensure your protégé has a fair chance at putting his or her new learning into practice. This may entail securing support or permissions from others who may affect the protégé's performance. A friend of ours tells the story of how an early mentor supplemented the mentoring sessions by arranging for the protégé to attend a two-day workshop with a renowned guru in the field. But the mentor did not stop there. When the protégé returned enthusiastic and full of new ideas, she was surprised to get a call from the president of the company inviting her to lunch to discuss how she might implement what she had learned. The president's interest gave her courage to push against initial resistance of her colleagues. She learned a few years later that her mentor had suggested to the president that he give ear to her new learnings.

Be Vigilant for Obstacles to Learning

The late Geary Rummler was fond of saying, "You can take highly motivated, well-trained employees, put them in a lousy system, and the system will win every time." Effective learning results can become ineffective performance results if the protégé enters a system, process, or unit that punishes—or simply does not encourage—the newly acquired skills. A crucial part of your role is to be ever vigilant for obstacles that undermine the learning acquired through your mentoring.

Think of your protégé's learning as a newly planted tree. In time the tree will have deep roots and a hardy resistance to wind, disease, and extreme temperatures. But as a sapling, it is particularly vulnerable. It must be supported, protected, and meticulously cared for until it can fend for itself. And it takes time and patience. In the words of the old adage, "You don't need to pull the tree up by the roots every five minutes to see if it's still growing and traumatize it." So it is with a protégé. As a novice, he is still learning, and his new skills are weak and unstable. Defending new behavior against external pressures to go back to the old way is challenging. Protégés need mentors to aid in their struggle to sustain new skills.

Several years ago one of us consulted with a large high-tech firm eager to make customer service its claim to fame. The CEO decided that everyone on the front line would be assigned a mentor to meet with weekly for an hour to talk about customer-service challenges. Managers were given mentoring training, procedures were put in place to ensure the weekly mentor-protégé meetings occurred, and everyone was happy with the initial results. In fact, customer service scores made significant jumps as frontline employees, armed with enhanced skills and newfound support, turned indifference into enthusiasm.

Six months into the mentoring project, the CEO decided to delegate the system-wide effort to someone in a staff role. It signaled a dampening of commitment. Managers were pressured to trim their one-hour sessions to thirty minutes; then weekly became monthly. As results declined and customer satisfaction scores turned downward, pressure was put on the staff leader to "fix it." The solution was to take an iron-fist approach to paperwork completion. Early enthusiasm turned to cynicism and resentment. The company was acquired, the CEO was replaced, and the mentoring endeavor was replaced with more hard-line, cost-cutting efforts. You can imagine how the rest of the story played out.

Be an Advocate for Informal Learning

Being a great mentor includes fostering an environment that values and nurtures learning. This means advocating informal learning. And there are myriad ways to make learning a natural part of the work world.

A major consulting firm found that professional reading among employees increased when the firm installed magazine racks with professional journals in the lavatories. The firm's president discovered that surprisingly few journals were absent-mindedly removed, and employees began contributing their own copies of journals to which the firm did not subscribe. Comments like "Did you read that article about...?" were frequently interjected in staff meetings, which further reinforced the amount of informal learning through journal reading.

Company magazines, newsletters, and bulletin boards can also be a good source of learning for employees. Let your protégé know about valuable Internet links to tag as favorites for continuous learning. An insurance company found the most popular articles in its company magazine were interviews with executives, managers, and employees dealing with what their area was engaged in at the time. Done with clever layout and graphics, "to all employees" media can serve as a valuable but inexpensive way of fostering employee learning. The unit or company intranet can likewise be a great boon to learning.

Another approach to informal learning is cross-unit sharing. A large research and development company effectively employed this process. Once a month a work group met for breakfast with a group from a different part of the company. People downlink were provided access via the company intranet. Each unit would take thirty minutes to describe their function and current projects. The remaining thirty minutes was devoted to informal conversation among the work groups in a cocktail-party fashion. The company found the monthly hour-and-a-half breakfast gathering an effective way of increasing employee breadth and decreasing interunit conflict. A bank used a similar arrangement but added a tour of the respective work areas to the cross-unit sharing process. Allotting staff meeting time for people to report on what was learned at a major conference or following the completion of a workshop or course signals that learning is valued.

Learning that ends when the protégé bids adieu to the mentor is likely retained only until the protégé reaches the elevator. Given the shaky tentativeness of new learning, it is up to the mentor to come up with ways to help shelter, support, and nurture it until it "takes." Knowing how to eliminate barriers and erect supports to buttress the learner until habits are cemented and competencies are hardwired can go a long way to help the learning-transfer process for your protégé. Most important is to create a climate that prizes not only ongoing learning but also risk taking in the protégé's trying out new knowledge and skills back on the job.

22

"If You Want Something to Grow, Pour Champagne on It!"

Only the curious will learn and only the resolute overcome the obstacles to learning. The quest quotient has always excited me more than the intelligence quotient.

Eugene S. Wilson

What do Clint Eastwood in the movie *Million Dollar Baby,* Tom Cruise in *Jerry McGuire,* Sandra Bullock in *The Blind Side,* and Denzel Washington in *Remember the Titans* have in common? They are all characters who supported and sought the best in others, even in their darkest hours. Growing champions isn't necessarily about applause, cheers, or approval. All of those actions may be present, but championing makes someone feel treasured, not just appreciated. They use the philosophy first espoused by Carol Lavin Bernick, chair of a skin beauty products manufacturer, "If you want something to grow, pour champagne on it."

Great mentors focus on the effect they are trying to create, not on the set of tasks they are supposed to "check off." It's much like empowerment. Leaders don't embed power; they remove the barriers to power. They don't motivate; they create conditions that help employees motivate themselves. In much the same way, great mentors don't merely recognize or appreciate; they nourish spirit by whatever means necessary. The by-products of great championing are enhanced employee self-esteem, confidence, pride, and commitment. Champion growers focus more on the outcome of their efforts and less on the process used.

Advocate, Don't Just Celebrate

Did you ever have someone who believed in you unconditionally even though you didn't feel you deserved such backing? A celebrator recognizes and affirms what you accomplish, but a grower of champions shows respect and admiration for who you are and believes in you when others may have written you off. A grower of champions campaigns on your behalf, backs you against all odds, and defends you against all foes. The concept of mentor as a grower of champions goes far beyond the usual affirmation. Mentors as champion growers do not view their role as cheerleaders; they see themselves more as stewards of reputation.

Affirm Responsible Freedom

Learning takes risks, and risk taking involves breaking patterns and abandoning "the way we've always done it." To get effective protégé growth, it is important to affirm appropriate risk taking—not foolhardy recklessness. One high-tech company gives its annual "green weenie" award to the individual who, while clearly pursuing excellence, made a mistake that produced the greatest organizational learning and improvement.

Value Learning Outcomes, Not Just the Great Effort

A happy-go-lucky nurse won the hearts of her patients by bringing them flowers grown in her garden and cookies baked in her oven. They raved to managers about her sunny disposition and special generosity. She was the recipient of a special recognition at the annual awards banquet to the sharp displeasure of her coworkers. While all acknowledged her special way with patients, they were quick to point out her sloppy paperwork, inconsistent hand washing, and unwillingness to pull her weight on tasks they all shared. All those poor practices adversely impacted the healthcare outcome but were out of sight of her adoring fans. Effective affirmation practices require performance on "the basics" to be at least at expected levels. We all enjoy friendly flight attendants, but the plane must still land in the right city!

Align Advocacy with Vision

When famed tennis coach Mike Estep talks about his role as the coach of tennis great Martina Navratilova, he focuses on bringing out the very best in his client. He also speaks of elevating her playing to match the greatness of the game itself. Tiger Woods credits his late father, Earl, with helping him think about making an impact on the world beyond golf and his awe-inspiring athletic feats. And who could miss the influence of Richard Williams on his tennis-great daughters Serena and Venus Williams. Mike Estep, Richard Williams, and Earl Woods, great champion growers all, zeroed in on a vision of greatness that was much more than the sum of the competitor and the contest. Champion growers are committed to a vision and use it as a tool, not only to direct and align performance, but to affirm and motivate protégés as well.

Champion Growers Don't "Affirm Conditionally"

Conditional affirmation ("Annabeth, you're doing a great job, but...") turns the receiver deaf to the positive piece of the commentary. And if the critique carries parental tones, power and status issues are also raised. So what do the best leaders do? They separate praise and criticism. If your goal is to praise, then praise. If your goal is to criticize, then criticize. Mixing the two in the same sentence or session can turn a confirming pat on the back into a controlling kick in the pants.

The word "champion" comes from the Latin word *campio* which means "trial by combat." The implication is that champions are not "the lucky few"; they are those who have been tested in adversity or challenge and found to be with substance. When our fathers labeled such a person "someone who came from great stock," they meant a person of character as well as excellence, not just someone with talent or tenacity. Mentors who grow champions zero in on surfacing the best, nurturing the best, and affirming the best.

Archeologists excavating the pyramids discovered wheat seeds that dated back to around 2500 BC. As in the tradition of antiquity, the seeds were there for the dead pharaoh to eat if he got hungry. The find was important because it would enable scientists to determine what variety of wheat was in use in the ancient world and could be invaluable for engineering new types of wheat. Out of curiosity, the scientists planted the 4,500-year-old wheat seed in fertile soil and an amazing thing happened. The wheat seeds grew! In the end, the goal of the mentoring relationship is to ensure that in the end "the wheat seeds grow!"

23

Managing Sweet Sorrow

Life after Mentoring

Every path but your own is the path of fate. Keep on your own track, then.

Henry David Thoreau

Effective mentoring relationships are rich, engaging, and intimate. But all such arrangements must come to an end, and no matter how hard we may try to avoid it, every ending has a bittersweet dimension. As Shakespeare so eloquently reminds us, "Parting is such sweet sorrow." As you and your protégé reach the end of your partnership, how do you manage "farewell" with a focus on "well"?

Going for Growth

You would be remiss in your duties as a mentor if you made the parting an occasion for lingering regret. Healthy mentoring relationships use separation as a tool for growth. Below are several ideas for ending a mentoring relationship gracefully and constructively.

Celebrate with Fanfare and Stories

Celebration need not be a party with band and banner; it can be as simple as a special meal together, a drink after work, a peaceful walk in a nearby park. The point of celebration, however, is to mark the end of the mentoring relationship. Celebration is a rite of passage, a powerful symbol of closure and of moving on to the next learning plateau.

A manager for a well-known West Coast software manufacturer mentioned that he was getting reports from other managers that supervisors who transferred from his department seemed to take longer than usual to adjust to their new supervisory roles. It was beginning to hurt his reputation within the organization as a supplier of competent talent. When he was asked to play back in reverse the events leading from his supervision to their new roles, it quickly became clear that their relationships with him never came to a formal end—they simply stopped. Later, when he began including the ritual of a celebrative closure on their last day under his supervision, the adjustment problems vanished.

Celebration should be rich in compliments and stories, laughter and joy. Your protégé graduate needs your blessing more than your brilliance, your good wishes more than your warnings. Avoid the temptation to lay on one last caution. Your kindest contribution will be a solid sendoff with gifts of confidence, compassion, and consideration.

Solidify Learning with Nostalgia

Lace your final meetings with opportunities to remember, reflect, and refocus. Let your recall questions bridge the discussion toward the future; merely reminiscing can mire the meeting in melancholy. Listen to your protégé with the devotion you would give your mentor. Honor your mature protégé with respect and recognition.

Let Time Pass before Follow-Up

The quickest route to delivering a message of dependence is to follow up with a protégé too soon after departure. Wait a week or more before calling or visiting. Setting your relationship free takes space and time. Should you follow up at all? Absolutely! Partners follow up on partners. The key is, not too quickly. Allow weaning time.

Let your protégé be his or her own person. There may be times when a former protégé is being honored and you will feel the urge to share the limelight. We know a professor who always wanted to share the credit when one of his students achieved some award. While pride was obviously a part of his response—"I was his major professor"—the action tended to keep his former protégé stuck in the "I'm still his student" position. Let go. Move on. Celebrate the past but concentrate on the future.

Just as rapport building is crucial to the beginning of a mentoring relationship, a sense of adjournment is equally important at its end. Letting go is rarely comfortable, but it's necessary if the protégé is to flourish and continue to grow out of the mentor's shadow. In the final analysis, the upper limit of growing is "grown," implying closure and culmination. Mark the moment by managing adjournment as a visible expression of achievement and happiness.

24

Fly High, Dive Deep

An Interview with Fred Hassan,
Managing Director and Partner
at Warburg Pincus, LLC

**How would you characterize or describe your most important
mentor?**

My most important mentor was a gentleman who hired me for
my first job in the pharmaceutical industry. He was a very senior
executive. He was vice president of finance and a very knowl-
edgeable and good person.

**What were the traits you found most instrumental to your
mentor's work with you?**

First of all, he was caring. He cared to build people around
him. He cared to build a team, so the team could also mentor
each other. He created this mentoring atmosphere, which was
extremely helpful. Secondly, he was very competent. He was always challenging himself and the rest of us to get better at what
we were doing. I started my career in corporate planning, which

was a very important part of the company. He encouraged us to be open-minded and aggressive with our thinking. As a result of that, I learned to be much more focused on changing things and not accepting status quo as the way to go. Lastly, he was a good friend. He mentored in a very informal style, which was very helpful to me. If someone puts you at ease, is not always trying to impress, then it is easier for the mentoring to occur. The more formal the atmosphere, the less easy it is for the mentoring to occur because then people are more concerned about other matters beyond mentoring.

What is one example or incident or illustration of how this person was helpful to you?

We were at a retreat in the Pocono Mountains in New Jersey in 1973. We were talking about lots of things, including complaining about the hotel, which was not the best. He said that in business life we should be like a seagull, which means you fly high so you can see the environment and the fish, and you also have to be able to dive and get in deep to catch the fish. He emphasized the importance of having the ability to see the big picture, and also get very detailed-oriented and execution-oriented. It was a tremendous comment, which I remind myself of again and again, that I need to be hands-on at times and I need to be conceptual at times. Some people are very good at seeing things, but they don't get the job done. Others are very focused on getting it done, but they don't see the right things to do. My mentor taught me that the seagull sees the opportunity and then dives in to capture the opportunity.

What advice or feedback did this person provide that was helpful to you?

My mentor told me that I should play to my strengths. He saw in me a person who was very good at running operations. (At the time I was in a staff function.) The fact that he said this to me meant a lot to me, and after that I accepted a job that went sideways for a while, but in the end was very helpful toward the positions I've had where I get to influence and lead people. It started with him saying that I need to play to my strengths. Now when I mentor people or hire them, I ask myself, are they playing to their strengths or will they be playing to their strengths if they get a particular job? We are all good at something; the key is to fit to the right opportunity. A great mentor helps us discover what our strengths are sooner than we might discover them on our own.

PART 6

SPECIAL CONDITIONS

I believe that we are here for each other, not against each other. Everything comes from an understanding that you are a gift in my life—whoever you are, whatever our differences.

John Denver

Mentoring is rarely the simple, cooperative experience the Jack and Tracy story has demonstrated. Mentoring often carries special challenges that test the skill of the mentor and try the patience of the protégé. Consider this section a special overlay for everything thus far covered in the book.

Two special conditions particularly affect the quality of the mentoring relationship: the players and the playground! In the chapter on unholy alliances, we will explore several peculiar player conditions: peer-to-peer mentoring, mentoring a person at a higher position, and mentoring a person who is sufficiently "different" to cause either of you anxiety. The most common differences are those at the core of most organizations' quest for diversity—gender, race/ethnicity, and creed. In our discussion, "creed" will be used to cover a host of differences...an extreme conservative mentoring an extreme liberal, people of different sexual orientations, or a New York urbanite mentoring a South Georgia ruralite.

The core issue in unholy alliances is the fact that they *may* (not will) raise anxiety or apprehension in the mentor or protégé. When a special condition is discovered or acknowledged (it may be obvious), it is up to the mentor to raise the issue and attempt to gauge whether it is a source of anxiety. How that surfacing occurs can strongly influence the level of candor likely to be used in the joint exploration.

The second type of special condition concerns the playground—the setting or context in which the mentoring relationship happens. Three conditions will be dissected: mentoring in a fast-paced world, mentoring when mentor and protégé are in different locations, and mentoring with the support or assistance of a nonhuman tool or resource. The first two—called white-water mentoring and remote mentoring—are hallmarks of the contemporary work world.

25

Unholy Alliances
Mentoring in Precarious Relationships

Humility leads to strength and not to weakness. It is the highest form of self-respect.

John McCloy

Mentoring is often about two relatively similar people—a wiser mentor and an eager-to-learn protégé—brought together for the facilitation of growth. However, that endeavor takes on a graver tone when the interpersonal relationship between mentor and protégé is dramatically outside the norm. Unholy alliances put a special pressure on the mentor. They likewise place unusual anxiety on the protégé.

The chances a protégé would be the offspring of a mentor in today's world of enterprise is not that rare, especially in private companies. It is symbolic of the diversity found in today's workplaces. It figuratively telegraphs the existence of many varieties of precarious relationships that can challenge the partnering aim of mentoring.

Trading Power for Respect:
When Pupils Are Peers

When Chip's son was a fourth-grader, he came home one day and announced that he had a new teacher assistant.

"Did your old teacher assistant leave?" Chip asked.

"No," he replied, "Mrs. Greer is still there."

"What's your new teacher assistant's name?" Chip asked.

Without looking up from kicking his soccer ball, he responded matter-of-factly: "Tommy."

Chip instantly knew this was weird. Fourth-graders don't refer to their teachers by their first names. Tenth-graders use teachers' first names as an act of rebellion; twelfth-graders do it to sound grown up and cool. But most fourth-graders are not interested in being rebellious or cool.

As it turned out, Tommy was a sixth-grader and a part of a cross-age education effort to let older students tutor younger students. The concept was that elementary students often respond better to older peers than to a teacher, and placing teaching responsibility on the older students increased their growth as well.

Four months into Chip's son's experience, he asked how his son and Tommy were doing. "He's not a helper anymore," he replied. Chip decided to keep his mouth closed to see if he would fill him in. He continued, "Tommy thought he knew more about math than me. And when I started getting answers faster than he did, he got really mad. He started calling me names. Mrs. Greer heard him and took his job away from him."

Peer mentoring poses special challenges no matter what the setting. Resistance is always an obstacle in mentoring, and it becomes especially acute when the mentor and protégé are peers. Most peer-mentors are painfully aware of how labels like "smart aleck" and "know-it-all" stick to those who profess to have wisdom they want to share. How do you make peer mentoring work when resistance so easily raises its ugly head? Hold that question while we consider another challenging situation.

Mentoring THE BOSS

How do you mentor someone in a higher position? The most common answer you will hear to that question is, "Very carefully!"

As we have explored throughout this book, risk taking is tantamount to growth, and mixing learning and power produces a concoction that is typically risk-averse. This mixture is particularly powerful when mentoring a person in a higher position. Yet more and more organizations are, for example, asking younger employees who hold lower positions in the organization but possess key skills to be mentors to leaders in higher positions who need those skills. Consider, for example, the computer-illiterate CEO who asks the whizbang computer nerd in the bowels of the IT department, "Come up to mahogany row and teach me how to use this thing!"

Mentoring the boss can carry another unfortunate by-product. The protégé can quickly bear the brunt of resentment if seen as the "teacher's pet." Perceived favoritism can play havoc with an employee's position in an important peer group.

The general manager of a major New York hotel came from a section of that city not famous for interpersonal diplomacy. Wanting to soften her rather clipped, abrupt style, she sought the assistance of a charming front-desk supervisor. "The supervisor was thrilled I asked for her assistance," reported the GM. "But I could immediately sense some hesitation. After a bit of probing, I realized she was worried about being seen as someone trying to curry the favor of the boss. When I had asked her! So, at the next staff meeting I quelled her anxiety by announcing that I had *insisted* she be my mentor. 'And,' I told the staff, 'after trying to turn me down, she relented and agreed to help me out.' By adding a humorous touch to the announcement, I allayed any perception others might have that she might have been 'brownnosing the boss.'"

Humility First

Mentoring in challenging situations—with peers, people above, people who are different—requires an attitude of awe. Communicating that sense of wonderment is best done through an expression of raw, unedited humility. Humility is a special gift of managers who succeed as mentors. It is more than a gift in the case of peer, boss, and diversity mentoring—it's the key to the front door. If you start off by showing off your expertise, you're guaranteed to lose your noncaptive audience. When a boss is doing the mentoring, protégés think they have to listen, and perhaps even act interested—but peers will simply blow you off and not waste their time. Bosses in the protégé position know they rank above you—and have the right to not be engaged.

With anyone who is "different," humility turns fear into connection—but humility is not a synonym for apology. To be humble means to be unassuming and egoless, acting from the soul without adding anything. You can be both humble and confident.

Ask Lots of Questions Up Front

Most protégés, when confronted with a mentor who does not fit the traditional mentor-protégé mold, show resistance at first: "What the heck could you teach me?" "Who appointed you Mister Know-It-All?" or "I'm just as good as you!" Just like mentors, protégés sometimes harbor the notion that mentors should be superior. Any deviation from the traditional order of things makes them nervous. A crucial first step is to allay protégé anxieties and deal with the resistance.

One way to deal with resistance is to put enormous focus, energy, and attention on the protégé at the start of the relationship. Demonstrate dramatic listening. Forget about reciprocity for a while. Let the interest be one-sided—yours in the protégé. You'll get your turn later. Think of it this way: every time you ask a question of the protégé, you gain a point. Every time you make a statement, you lose a point. And every time you make a statement about your background, your interest, your experience, or your anything, you lose five points. Get as many points as you can in the first ten minutes of the encounter.

Never Resist Resistance

One of the greatest lessons students of judo learn is never to resist resistance; instead, they learn to divert the energy of resistance to other uses. When you meet resistance with resistance, the barriers become more rigid, the heels of opposition dig deeper into the ground of power, and growth comes to a screeching halt.

Judo teaches students to use their opponent's energy by joining it and guiding it to a new place. Similarly, in a mentoring situation, you will do better to accept the learner's resistance and seek to learn from it. Pursue it, solicit it, and get it into the light of day by showing no fear of it. Treat conflict as a neutral force that can be applied to learning. Accept it as unresolved tension that needs to be understood to be channeled in a positive direction.

Strive for Reciprocal Learning

Pursue equality in your relationship. Learning happens best when it occurs on a level playing field. If your protégé sees you as a fellow learner (rather than as an "I'll show you" smarty-pants), there is greater potential for a partnership. With partnership come acceptance, joint contribution, and growth.

Seek something your protégé knows that you would like to learn, and couple your mentoring with being a protégé to your protégé. Better still, pursue an area in which you both want to learn. Reciprocity is rarely a perfectly balanced fifty-fifty. Healthy relationships in all areas of life are sixty-forty one week and forty-sixty the next. Over time, however, the give-and-take clearly reflects a fair balance.

Mentoring People Who Are Very Different

Dances with Wolves was one of Kevin Costner's crowning movie achievements. Costner directed and played the lead role in the film based on the book by Michael Blake. It won seven Academy Awards, including best picture. It is the story of Lieutenant John Dunbar, an accidental Civil War hero who is given his choice of assignments after the war. He requests a solitary remote outpost, a rundown hut on the Western Plains in the middle of Indian Territory. In the late 1860s, the prejudicial view of Native Americans was that they were thieves and savages; Native Americans saw whites as a greedy inferior race with no reverence for nature and no skill with horses. If reciprocal learning was to occur in the face of such diversity, it would require a special approach.

Lieutenant Dunbar, after his first encounter with a representative of a nearby Sioux tribe, Kicking Bird, wrote in his diary that the man was confused and anxious but acknowledged the Indian "was a magnificent man." Kicking Bird, a wise medicine man, told the tribe elders, "The white man was brave and did not seem to be eager for war." The stage was set for openness to difference.

Find a Common Emotional Meeting Ground

When Dunbar and Kicking Bird sat together for the first time at Dunbar's solitary post in the middle of the plains, their language difference posed a major challenge: Dunbar did not speak Lakota; Kicking Bird did not speak English. The dilemma weighed heavy on both to find a way to begin to fashion any sort of connection. Finally, Lieutenant Dunbar got down on all fours, put a rolled up piece of clothing under his shirt creating a hump at his shoulders, and began to paw the ground. Wind in His Hair, one of Kicking Bird's associates, commented, "His mind is gone!" But then Kicking Bird realized Dunbar was mimicking a buffalo. "Tatunka, tatunka!" Kicking Bird explained. Dunbar poorly pronounced the Lakota word back and exclaimed, "Yes, yes, buffalo, buffalo."

This time Kicking Bird poorly pronounced the English word back, and a connection was suddenly forged. They both laughed.

As Kicking Bird and the accompanying braves left Dunbar's solitary post to return to their own camp, Dunbar said to himself: "Nothing I have been told about these people is correct. They are not thieves or beggars. They are not the bogeymen they are made out to be. On the contrary, they are polite guests and I enjoy their humor." Mentoring between people with major differences begins with finding a common emotional meeting ground.

Give a Gift That Is Important to You

On the second visit, Kicking Bird brought Dunbar a large buffalo-skin blanket. It was a cherished prize for the Sioux Indians, who followed large herds of buffalo for food and clothing. With hard winters, Kicking Bird rightly predicted Dunbar was ill-supplied with clothing that would properly protect from the cold. Dunbar treated Kicking Bird with coffee with sugar. The Kicking Bird delegation of braves sat patiently as Dunbar ground the coffee and put it in their cups. None were impressed with the taste until Dunbar added ground sugar, something they had never seen. Each left with a tin cup, a bag of coffee, and a bag of sugar. For the first time, they waved as they left. Begin the mentoring encounter with a gift that is important to you that might be shared with the protégé. Guessing at what might be important to them could backfire and lead to an awkward start.

Sharing Who You Are, Not Just What You Want

The first time Lieutenant Dunbar was invited to the Sioux encampment for a private meeting with Kicking Bird, the two were joined by Stands With a Fist, a white woman who as a child had lost her entire family and been raised by the Sioux. Her English was very rusty as she struggled to serve as interpreter to the two. Immediately, Kicking Bird wanted to know why the military outpost was there and when other white men might come. But Stands With a Fist intervened, saying that personal introductions should come first. Even though the two men had had several encounters, this was the first time an interpreter had enabled them to communicate. And once each knew the other's name, a true relationship began. As Dunbar left to return to his hut, he said to himself: "They are people so eager to laugh, so devoted to family, so dedicated to each other. The only word that comes to mind is 'harmony.'" Mentoring at its finest is a harmonious partnership between two people who share who they are, not just what they want of each other.

Mentoring in precarious relationships offers both special rewards and special challenges. The secret to success lies in taking what is ostensibly a unique relationship and managing the exchange of wisdom so that it maintains and honors equality. Focusing on humility, sincere consideration, authentic affirmation, and balance can foster an exchange that brings significant growth to both mentor and protégé.

26

Arduous Alliances
Mentoring in Precarious Situations

*The only people who achieve much are those who want knowledge so badly that
they seek it while the conditions are still unfavorable. Favorable conditions never
come.*

C. S. Lewis

There are many learning alliances that are potentially arduous because of the precarious context in which the relationship is cast. We
will examine two situations: mentoring in a super-fast-paced milieu
and mentoring when the protégé is in a different location. We will
first examine white-water mentoring.

Mentoring on the Run: White-Water Wisdom

Speed is both the genie and the ogre for today's supervisors. Some
thrive on it; some long for the olden days. Like it or not, however,
warp speed (a.k.a. cycle time, just in time, or out of time) is a trade-
mark of our unpredictable work environments.

Dubbed "permanent white water" by Peter Vaill in *Managing
as a Performing Art,* the nature of today's business world challenges
the supervisor's coaching and mentoring responsibilities. There are

too many "I'll have to get back to you" responses to "Help me figure out how to" requests. The pressure to do wins out over the requirement to teach and learn. What can you do to coach on the run and still be effective? How can you keep up with the demands of the "Time's up!" moment while making sure protégés receive the one-on-one attention, support, and tutelage they need to avoid skill obsolescence? Below are three tips for navigating through the white water.

Take Time for Learner Readiness

Great athletes always warm up, no matter how short the event. Under time pressure, many mentors tend to give short shrift to ascertaining whether the protégé is ready to learn. Lines like "Let me get right to the punch line" risk neglecting the protégé's learning needs and leaving him overwhelmed and confused. Remember the old truism that longer planning time results in shorter implementation time, and less time overall? The same is true for learning.

No matter how little time you have for teaching, always take time to find out (1) the employee's immediate learning needs and goals ("What do you need to learn?"), (2) any pressing concerns that might affect *how* you would help, and (3) the employee's ideas on how you might be most helpful.

Beware of "Let Me Just Show You How!"

Good mentors don't rescue, they support. The temptation of most leaders under the gun is to resort to demonstration rather than supportive direction. The real motivation behind "Let me just show you how" is to get the work out while ostensibly helping the employee learn. This approach may boost short-term performance, but long-term proficiency suffers.

Does this mean that the mentor should never demonstrate a procedure? Of course not. The employee can often benefit from being shown how as she learns to do it for herself. But before you touch the keyboard, equipment, or report, ask yourself two questions: (1) Am I rescuing myself or supporting her? and (2) Will my demonstration increase or decrease independence?

Build Strong Parts Rather Than Weak Wholes

You're ten minutes away from rushing out the door to go to an important all-day meeting. One of your employees walks into your cubicle and announces, "I'm stuck on this new M60 filterator process you asked me to learn. Can you spare a few minutes to help me figure it out?" You know that it will actually take thirty or forty minutes to explain adequately; the employee has received only an overview orientation. Being late to the meeting is not an option, but you want some M60 performance from this protégé today. What do you do?

Many mentors would give a ten-minute condensation of the forty-minute lesson and hope the employee could then muddle though. The result of such a hit-and-run approach is likely to be complete confusion; an hour after you're gone, the employee will remember only a blur. A better approach is to identify the ten-minute part of your forty-minute lesson that is most crucial to getting started and cover that part thoroughly. Solid learning on a key part will create confident momentum and enable the protégé to learn the rest on his or her own. Competence in a limited area is better than vague awareness of the whole.

The futurists tell us that the days of "Take your time!" are over for the business world; a "Time's up!" pace, whether blessing or curse, is now essential to success. At the same time, employees must remain up to date on mastery of new skills. Superior mentors will be those who can competently tutor on the run.

Mentoring Long Distance: Remote Learning

Marshall sat in the back row of a large, dimly lit auditorium filled with managers from a software company being treated to the last million-slide presentation of the day. Earlier he had spoken to this audience about the myths, merits, and methods of mentoring and coaching. A bright young systems engineer manager sitting three people to his right passed Marshall a napkin with a handwritten note: "Do you have any suggestions on how I can mentor my people in Guam, Paris, and San Juan? They feel ignored and I feel guilty."

With seventeen slides, polite applause, and the speaker's closing remarks to go, Marshall had a little time to think. He can't remember now much about what he said—she seemed satisfied—but he can remember being struck by the realization that this dilemma is now commonplace.

We live in an era of self-directed work. Widening spans of control, downsizing, and rising numbers of employees without direct supervision have compelled leaders to supervise more and more at arm's length. Weak bosses feel relieved, their subordinates freed; but strong leaders can feel guilty and their subordinates ignored. The systems engineer's dilemma is becoming familiar to more and more leaders: How do you mentor when you're not there, and won't be for a while? How do you mentor long distance?

Create a Buddy System on Site

When you're not there, you're not there. It's important, therefore, to shore up other avenues for growth. A too-often-overlooked resource is the wisdom of peers. This doesn't mean going back to the old "Watch Nellie" style of yesteryear. A true buddy system carefully matches protégé learning needs with the best colleague wisdom. To be effective, the buddy system must be based not just on availability but on purposeful matchmaking: personality matching, skill matching, and priority matching.

So how do I get Jane to mentor John on the Tillich technique when Jane and John are peers? First, hold Jane accountable for being supportive and available to mentor. Second, hold John accountable for seeking out Jane and learning the Tillich technique. Be sure to praise Jane for her mentoring, John for learning Tillich.

Easier said than done? Of course; isn't it always? Buddy systems work when we spend the effort to make them work. They require resources—especially time. Telling Jane to mentor John is great, but not if you don't cut Jane enough slack in her other duties.

Provide Learning Care Packages

Chip was working with a major hotel chain, teaching a part of their weeklong Lodging Leadership program. The participants were general managers from hotels around the world. It was lunchtime midweek, and Steve, one of the program participants from a hotel in New Orleans, received a large package. Many people gathered around as Steve opened the surprise. The package was filled with an assortment of items: a coffee mug, a favorite candy bar, a flash drive, a package of pencils, a note pad, an inexpensive pair of reading glasses, sleeping pills, playing cards. It was from all the employees in his hotel back home. He was visibly moved. The practicality of the items was irrelevant; he had been remembered—and valued! He was instantly reminded of his commitment to do his best for his people.

Part of mentoring long distance is letting the protégé experience your concern and caring in tangible ways. An article, a link to a helpful blog, a CD or book on a topic of interest or need, a special job aid, or an audiotape on a work-related topic can send a powerful message that the person is remembered—and valued! Give the protégé a subscription to a magazine important to his professional growth. Place him on the e-mail list for growth-oriented items coming from your office.

When you are on site with the protégé, make note of small items he may not have but would find useful. Stationery and supplies may be stockroom items that can be had for the asking; unique items may take a bit more thought and planning. Could he use a rubber stamp of his business address? Is there a user list to which you could helpfully add his name? How would the protégé react to getting a package of Post-it® notes with his name printed on them?

Care packages are limited only by your imagination; the best are those tailored to the protégé's individual needs, preferences, and situation.

Find Surrogate Mentors

When you can't be there in person, send an agent on your behalf. How many old B-grade war movies have you watched in which the hard-nosed general shows a surprising soft side by sending a valued expert in to assist? "The general asked me to drop by and see if I might be able to lend a hand!" It was usually a turning point in the movie. Learning agents are allies of growth; they can fill a gap, shore up a weakness, or simply lend confidence.

When considering people resources outside your organization, find an agent who has not just expertise but status. Providing the help of a person with both special resources and unique status can send a double message: I value you; I want to help you grow. It also can be a special treat for the agent you select.

Chip had the opportunity to consult a large northwestern bank as the designer and instructor of a two-day training program that would be taught to supervisors at various sites by a group of carefully selected managers. The program was designed and field-tested, and a series of train-the-trainer sessions was conducted. Linda was Chip's client and senior project leader; Phil was one of the handpicked managers chosen to teach this new course. Phil had been very successful in the train-the-trainer sessions.

One day Linda called. "I need your help and will gladly pay you for the day," she began. "Phil has a particularly difficult group next month on the other side of the state, and I think he'd feel a lot more confident if you could be there for his first day—sort of as his assistant."

Phil did great! He really didn't need any help. But the relief on his face was obvious when his "assistant" (Chip) arrived unexpectedly that morning an hour before his first participant appeared. It was fun watching Phil discover his own style for effectively teaching the new program.

Create a Self-Directed Learning Plan

"The most powerful contribution teachers can make to students," human resource development guru Leonard Nadler has said, "is to help learners become their own teachers." However, the gift of self-directed learning to the protégé can pose a threat to the mentor for whom letting go means feeling left out, unneeded, and under-valued. It takes great courage, compassion, and caring to let the bluebird teach itself to fly. Because it is counterintuitive to you as a caring mentor, you need to take steps to ease the transition.

Meet with your far-away protégé and establish a learning plan. (Tool #5 shows the key elements in a structured plan.) Check the protégé's progress at longer and longer intervals—once a month, then once every two months, then quarterly, and so forth. The goal is to wean *yourself* out of the process, not just the protégé. Make sure the strategies for learning use resources available to the protégé. Protégés who take responsibility for their own learning will show greater motivation. The old saw "If the student hasn't learned, the teacher hasn't taught" does *not* apply to adults. (It doesn't apply to children either, but that's another story.)

Learning cannot always be tied to a full-time, full-access re-lationship. Today's work world is far from stable, regular, or planned, but learning must continue if organizations are to adapt and compete. Tomorrow's master mentors will be enablers, not ex-perts; supporters, not smart persons. They will search beyond the old horizons to provide resources for protégés in Guam, Paris, and San Juan—as well as Galveston, Peoria, and Building Four.

What about E-Mentoring?

There was a time when mentoring via the cyberworld was a lot like a modern-day version of mentoring a pen pal—communication was via e-mail, making it a static, faceless conversation. The mobil-ity, speed, and ease of the Internet as a tool for "interlogue" are clearly worthwhile assets. However, without the capacity to read nonverbal information, there is great potential for misinformation and misinterpretation. Without accurate dialogue, understanding can suffer.

One study at UCLA indicated that up to 93 percent of communication effectiveness is determined by nonverbal cues. Another study found that the impact of a performance was determined 7 percent by the words used, 38 percent by voice quality, and 55 percent by the nonverbal communication.[1] Stripping the lion's share of the effectiveness features from communications with customers puts an enormous burden on those factors that are left.

The good news is that e-mentoring has evolved to reliance on technology that allows face-to-face encounters. Now, using connections such as Skype and Facetime, the mentor and protégé can simulate a live meeting. However, a few suggestions can make e-mentoring a richer discussion.

> **Share background information before the online sessions.** Since most e-mentoring sessions only show the other person's face, each lacks the context of the setting that might provide helpful clues about the other person.
>
> **Pace the conversation slower than normal.** Rapid conversation increases the likelihood of each person talking over the other and missing key information.
>
> **Use ear phones or speakers** to increase the depth of the sound, enabling you to hear subtleties in your protégé's voice.

Mentoring does not always happen in the secure routine of a stable work site. With the business environment becoming more chaotic, more globalized, and more dependent on technology, wise mentors learn to coach on the run, at a distance, using all the technology available to them. Granted, the pace of a protégé's learning may be different from the pace of work, but the realities of speed and the uncertainties of permanent white water still color the learning experience. Protégés should not be denied the help of their mentor just because they are physically inaccessible. Wise mentors adjust to the realities of place. They also embrace the power of technology.

27

Respect Everyone

An Interview with Frances Hesselbein, President and
CEO of the Frances Hesselbein Leadership Institute

**How would you characterize or describe your most important
mentor?**

It will surprise most people to learn that my most important
mentor was my grandmother and our mentoring began, con-
sciously, when I was eight years old.

Since the beginning of my career, I have had several influential fellow travelers—Peter Drucker, Marshall Goldsmith, John
W. Gardner—who have had a powerful and positive impact upon
my life and work, yet it was my grandmother's teachings that had
and continue to have this incredible influence and impact.

**What were the traits you found most instrumental in their work
with you?**

"Respect for all people" was the trait. The most significant lesson I learned from that trait became a compelling force in my life.

A second trait was the art of listening or, as Peter Drucker expanded it, "Think first, speak last," and "Ask, don't tell." My grandmother in the mountains of western Pennsylvania long ago lived and in her life shared these powerful qualities with a little girl growing up.

What is one example/incident/illustration of how they were helpful to you?

A powerful illustration story told to me by my grandmother, Mama Wicks, follows:

"Long ago, when your mother was eight years old, some days she and her little sisters would come home from school crying that the bad boys were chasing Mr. Yee and calling him bad names.

"Now in this little town was a Chinese laundry man, who lived alone in his small one-room laundry shed. Each week he picked up your grandfather's shirts and brought them back in a few days, washed, starched, ironed perfectly.

"Mr. Yee wore traditional Chinese dress—a long tunic, a cap with his hair in a queue.

The boys would chase him, teasing him, calling him, 'Chinky, Chinky Chinaman' and worse, and would try to pull his queue."

One day there was a knock on the kitchen door; my grandmother opened the door and there stood Mr. Yee, with a large package wrapped in newspaper in his arms. My grandmother said, "Oh, Mr. Yee, please come in. Won't you sit down?" Mr. Yee stood there, handed Mama Wicks the package, and said, "This is for you."

She opened the package and in it were two beautiful ancient Chinese vases. She said, "Mr. Yee—these are too valuable. I could not accept them." He said, "I want you to have them. I am going back home. They won't let me bring my wife and children here and I miss them too much, so I am going back to

China. The vases are all I brought with me. I want you to have them." My grandmother said, "Mr. Yee, why do you want me to have them?" He replied, "Mrs. Wicks, I have been in this town for ten years and you are the only one who ever called me 'Mr. Yee.'"

There were tears in his eyes as he said good-bye. And went back to China. Hearing the story, I cried my heart out in my grandmother's arms, for Mr. Yee.

That was long ago—the defining moment when I learned respect for all people, the defining moment that would stay with me, would shape my life with passion for diversity, for inclusion, respect, and civility.

When my grandmother died, she left a little note, "I want Frances to have the Chinese vases."

Today, they are in my living room, in Easton, Pennsylvania, on a shelf surrounded by a wall of books. I walk into my living room where the vases remind me of Mr. Yee and the lesson he and Mama Wicks taught me when I was eight years old, "respect for all people."

What advice or feedback did this person provide that was helpful to you?

Respect for all people.

"Look deeply into the eyes of the person speaking, listen to every word. Listen, smile, and show respect." "Good manners are essential. No matter what the message, the situation, we listen and respond with respect and, always good manners." Years later, Peter Drucker must have been on the same wavelength as Mama Wicks when he said, "Civility is the lubricating oil of effective organizations."

PART 7

THE MENTOR'S TOOLKIT

Any professional in the trades will tell you that having the expertise and experience is not sufficient for great performance. It also requires helpful tools. Tools not only are enablers—means to get the job done; they are also enhancers—devices that promote and support continuous improvement. In this section we provide several tools dedicated to mentor excellence.

Tool #1

Quick Tips for Mentors and Protégés

Mentoring on the run requires a few quick tips just to keep the edge honed and the skills sharp. The following quick tips are focused both on the mentor and the protégé. Remember, success comes through a partnership. Mentors need ideas for their side of the relationship just as much as protégés need ideas on the other side.

Tips for Being a Great Protégé

- Select a mentor who can help you be the best you can be, not one you think can help you get a promotion.

- Remember, you can sometimes learn more from people who are different than from people who are "just like you."

- Get crystal clear on your goals and expectations for a mentoring relationship.

- Communicate your goals and expectations in your first meeting.

- Mentoring is about learning, not looking good in front of your mentor. Be yourself and be willing to take risks and experiment with new skills and ideas.

- When your mentor gives you advice or feedback, work hard to hear it as a gift. Just because it may be painful does not mean it is not beneficial.

- If your mentoring relationship is not working like you hoped it would, clearly communicate your concerns to your mentor.

- Great mentoring relationships take two people—a partnership. Look in the mirror before you conclude a poor mentoring relationship is all about your mentor.

- Mentoring relationships are designed to be temporary. When you have met your mentoring goals, be willing to let the relationship end.

Tips for Being a Great Mentor

- Mentoring is about establishing a partnership that helps your protégé learn. It is not about your being an expert or the authority.

- Great mentors foster discovery, they don't instruct; thought-provoking questions are much more powerful than smart answers.

- Your protégé will learn more if you create a relationship that is safe and comfortable. Be authentic, open, and sincere.

- Your rank or position is your greatest liability—act more like a friend than a boss.

- Great listening comes from genuine curiosity and obvious attentiveness.

- Give feedback with a strong focus on the future, not a heavy rehash of the past.

- Mentoring is not just about what you say in a mentoring session; it is also about how you support your protégé after the session. Focus on helping your protégé transfer learning back to the workplace.

- If your mentoring relationship is not working like you hoped it would, clearly communicate your concerns to your protégé.

- Mentoring relationships are designed to be temporary. When your protégé has met his or her mentoring goals, be willing to let the relationship end.

Tool #2

Mentoring Competence Measures

Feedback is crucial to effective learning. Mentors need feedback just as much as protégés. To make the "getting feedback" process easier, we have included two versions of the Mentoring Competence Measure—one to be distributed to those you mentor, one that can be used as a self-assessment tool.

Mentoring Competence Measure

Person being rated: _____

1 = Strongly disagree; 3 = Disagree; 5 = Neither agree or disagree; 7 = Agree; 10 = Strongly Agree

1. He/she is an enthusiastic learner and shows
   an attitude of curiosity.   1 3 5 7 10

2. She/he demonstrates humility—always open and real.

                                                      1 3 5 7 10

3. He/she clearly links what is learned to a larger
   vision or purpose.   1 3 5 7 10

4. She/he helps me feel comfortable about taking
   appropriate risks.   1 3 5 7 10

5. If he/she makes a mistake, he/she admits it and takes
   responsibility for it.   1 3 5 7 10

6. She/he is an excellent listener, just as interested
   in standing in my shoes as making her/his own
   point of view known.   1 3 5 7 10

7. If he/she were to offer advice or a suggestion,
   it would be given with my interests at heart.   **1 3 5 7 10**

8. If we were in a discussion, I'm confident there
   would be a healthy "give and take," not a
   one-way lecture.   **1 3 5 7 10**

9. If I made a mistake, she/he would assume it
   was an honest error and help me learn from it.   **1 3 5 7 10**

10. He/she would give me feedback which
    was without judgment or any effort to make
    me feel guilty.   **1 3 5 7 10**

Total Score: _____.

90–100 = A first-class mentor; 80–89 = Good potential but has a few un-derdeveloped strengths; 70–79 = May resort to nonmentoring actions un-der stress; Below 70 = Might want to read *Managers as Mentors*...twice!!

Mentoring Competence Measure—Self-Assessment

1 = Strongly disagree; 3 = Disagree; 5 = Neither agree or disagree; 7 = Agree; 10 = Strongly Agree

1. My protégé would say I am an enthusiastic
   learner, always showing an attitude of curiosity.   1 3 5 7 10

2. My protégé would say I demonstrate humility—
   always open and real.   1 3 5 7 10

3. I clearly link what is learned to a larger
   vision and purpose.   1 3 5 7 10

4. My protégé would say I help him/her feel
   comfortable about taking appropriate risks.   1 3 5 7 10

5. If I make a mistake, I admit it and take responsibility for it.

   1 3 5 7 10

6. I am an excellent listener, just as interested
   in standing in my protégé's shoes as in making
   my own point of view known.   1 3 5 7 10

7. My protégé would say that if I offered advice or a
   suggestion, it would be given with his/her
   interests at heart.   1 3 5 7 10

8. If we were in a discussion, there would be a
   healthy "give and take," not a one-way lecture.   1 3 5 7 10

9. If my protégé made a mistake, I would assume
   it was an honest error and help him/her
   learn from it.   1 3 5 7 10

10. My protégé would say I would give him/her
    feedback which was without judgment or any
    effort to make him/her feel guilty.   1 3 5 7 10

Total Score: _____.

90–100 = A first-class mentor; 80–89 = Good potential but has a few underdeveloped strengths; 70–79 = May resort to nonmentoring actions under stress; Below 70 = Might want to read *Managers as Mentors* . . . twice!!

Tool #3

Mentoring FAQs

Since this is the "instruction manual" component to this book, we thought it would be helpful to include some of the "Frequently Asked Questions" we get when facilitating workshops on mentoring and coaching.

1. What are the challenges of the protégé being mentored by his or her supervisor?

We believe bosses should mentor those who are their subordinates. However, as we earlier stated, it is uniquely challenging carrying out an "insight" goal from an "in-charge" role. Since supervisors typically have a "performance assessor" role, protégés can be more reluctant to take growth-enhancing risks knowing the observer of their mistakes and blunders along the path to mastery will at some point be completing their report card. We have an important suggestion. We would encourage all supervisors to transit to a clear performance-based evaluation process.

2. Should you use personality tests (Myers Briggs, FIRO-B, DISC, etc.) to match mentors with protégés?

The plus side of using personality tests is to put people with similar styles together. While this matchmaking can clearly enhance comfort, it does little to help people learn from their differences. Another challenge is the ease with which people get subtly "encouraged" to take an instrument that reveals aspects about them they might prefer to keep private...particularly at the beginning of a relationship. We would encourage caution about using personality tests as a tool to put relationships together.

3. Where is the best place to hold a mentoring session?

Wherever the two people can best have focus and create a partnership relationship. Place is not the issue—privacy, quiet, and equality are. We have had highly successful mentoring sessions on a park bench, in a boat, or on a long walk. Focus on the conditions, not on the location.

4. What is the best time of day to hold a mentoring session?

The best time of day to hold a mentoring session is the time you are best able to ensure focus, privacy, and an egalitarian setting. What time has the best chance of being interruption-free? What time will both mentor and protégé be fresh and alert? What time favors both parties, not just one person?

5. What do I do if I don't personally like my protégé?

Before you turn this into a personality contest, ask yourself the following: Is your lack of affinity going to adversely impact your capacity to be a good mentor? Are your feelings more about you and less about the chemistry between you? Do you lack respect for your protégé's potential? Will your feelings rob you of your ability to be enthusiastic about the learning? If you answered "yes" to any of the questions above, reconsider proceeding. Be up-front with your protégé and offer to help him or her secure a better match.

6. My protégé and I do not get along. What should we do?

Find a shadow mentor who is skilled at interpersonal relationships. Ask the shadow mentor to sit in on one of your mentoring sessions and provide the two of you helpful feedback about ways to improve your relationship. Videotape your session and watch it together—as if you are watching someone else. Work together to find solutions to your conflicts. Remember, this is a partnership. Learning together is a vital part of what makes it work.

7. We are getting ready to start a mentoring program in our organization. What are your recommendations to ensure its success?

Be forewarned that most mentoring programs fail! As soon as it becomes a part of the bureaucracy with rules, procedures, and forms, you will hear the death knell of ineffectiveness. Instead, think about how to make mentoring a natural part of the organization. Are mentors trained to be mentors? Are mentors given adequate time and resources to mentor? Are good mentors recognized and rewarded for being effective mentors? Are the fruits of good mentoring recognized as a virtue in the organization? Are leaders selected because of their track record of mentoring? All these are much better ways to make mentoring a part of the DNA of the organization.

8. What are better words for "mentoring"? "Protégé" sounds too academic. And "mentor" is not a good word in our organization due to a previous failed attempt at a program.

Labels can be important, especially at the beginning when a mentoring initiative is building its reputation. Some organizations use "mentee" as the target of the mentoring effort and "learning coach" instead of "mentor." Some organizations do not label either party but focus on the name of the relationship—like "learning encounter" or even "mastery meeting."

9. Should the mentor and protégé have some common interests to help with rapport?

Again, the focus should be on creating a partnership. Common interests can indeed be a tool for rapport. But dissimilar interests and an obvious curiosity to learn about an interest other than your own can be a more effective model for a learning partnership. "I understand you are an avid hunter. I am an animal rights activist. It would be my hope to learn more about what you enjoy about deer hunting. Perhaps I might share some of my thoughts about animal rights. I am excited about what we can learn from each other."

10. What are the most frequent mistakes made by inexperienced mentors?

Perhaps the most frequent mistake is assuming the mentor's role is to transmit wisdom rather than foster discovery and nurture insight. Remember our panning-for-gold example in the opening of this book? The gold lies under sand and black mud. While the mentor can give guidance, it is the person holding the pan that finds the gold.

Tool #4

More Reading on Mentoring

We are often asked to suggest helpful books on mentoring. Below are ten recommendations.

Ensher, Ellen A., and Susan E. Murphy. *Power Mentoring: How Successful Mentors and Protégés Get the Most Out of Their Relationships*. San Francisco: Jossey-Bass, 2005.

Goldsmith, Marshall, Beverly Kaye, and Ken Shelton, eds. *Learn Like a Leader: Today's Top Leaders Share Their Learning Journeys*. Boston: Nicholas Brealey Publishing, 2010.

Huang, Chungliang A. *Mentoring: The Tao of Giving and Receiving Wisdom*. New York: HarperCollins, 1995.

Johnson, W. Brad, and Charles R. Ridley. *The Elements of Mentoring*. New York: Palgrave Macmillan, 2004.

Kaye, Beverly, and Julie Winkle Giulioni. *Help Them Grow or Watch Them Go: Career Conversations Employees Want*. San Francisco: Berrett-Koehler, 2012.

Maxwell, John C. *Mentoring 101: What Every Leader Needs to Know*. Nashville: Thomas Nelson, 2008.

Murray, Margo. *Beyond the Myths and Magic of Mentoring: How To Facilitate a Successful Mentoring Process*. San Francisco: Jossey-Bass, 2001.

Senge, Peter M. *The Fifth Discipline: The Art and Practice of the Learning Organization*. New York: Doubleday, 1990.

Zachary, Lois J. *Creating a Mentoring Culture: The Organization's Guide*. San Francisco: Jossey-Bass, 2005.

Zachary, Lois J. *The Mentor's Guide: Facilitating Effective Learning Relationships*, 2nd ed. San Francisco: Jossey-Bass, 2012.

Tool #5

Elements of a Learning Plan

1. **My learning goal is:** (e.g., I would like to develop an effective cus-
    tomer-service survey for the customers in my area of responsibility.)

    _____

    _____

2. **Resources I will likely require:** (e.g., I will need to talk with
    the general manager at the site, review the marketing research
    section at the library, call the customer service departments of
    three well-known marketing research consulting firms, etc.)

    _____

    _____

3. **People I know who can assist me:** (e.g., I need to talk with our
    organization's marketing research director.)

    _____

    _____

4. **Barriers I am likely to encounter and how I might overcome
    them:** (e.g., I have an outage report due that I need to delegate
    to Sam; the two-hour catering meeting needs to be shortened to
    one hour and everyone notified; etc.)

    _____

    _____

5. **Timetable I expect to use in achieving my objective:**

    _____

    _____

6. **Check-offs with my manager:** (dates and times)

    _____

    _____

7. **Other relevant notes on my learning plan:**

    _____

    _____

Tool # 6

The Eagle: An Inspirational Story

Our final tool is a poignant story about mentoring found in nature. Its primary purpose is to inspire you as it did us.

The eagle gently coaxed her offspring toward the edge of the nest. Her heart quivered with conflicting emotions as she felt their resistance to her persistent nudging. "Why does the thrill of soaring have to begin with the fear of falling?" she thought. This ageless question was still unanswered for her.

As in the tradition of the species, her nest was located high on the shelf of a sheer rock face. Below there was nothing but air to support the wings of each child. "Is it possible that this time it will not work?" she thought. Despite her fears, the eagle knew it was time. Her parental mission was all but complete. There remained one final task—the push.

The eagle drew courage from an innate wisdom. Until her children discovered their wings, there was no purpose for their lives. Until they learned how to soar, they would fail to understand the privilege it was to have been born. The push was the greatest gift she had to offer. It was her supreme act of love. And, so one by one she pushed them . . . and they flew!

David McNally

"The Eagle" is the gift of David McNally from his book *Even Eagles Need a Push* (NY, Dell Publishing, 1990, p. xiv). He has also written (with Mac Anderson) *The Push: Unleashing the Power of Encouragement*. Other works are available at www.davidmcnally.com and www.simpletruths.com

Notes

Beginning Our Journey
1. Peter Senge, *The Fifth Discipline: The Art and Practice of the Learning Organization* (New York: Doubleday, 1990).
2. Carlos Castaneda, *The Teachings of Don Juan: A Yaqui Way of Knowledge* (Berkeley: University of California Press, 1968).
3. Ram Dass (Richard Alpert), *The Only Dance There Is* (Garden City, NY: Anchor Press, 1974).

Chapter 1   Panning for Insight
1. Malcolm Knowles, *The Adult Learner: A Neglected Species*, 4th ed. (Houston: Gulf Publishing, 1990), 32.

Chapter 3   Assessing Your Mentoring Talents
1. The FIRO-B® instrument is distributed by Consulting Psychologists Press, CPP, Inc., 1055 Joaquin Road, Ste. 200, Mountain View, CA 94043; (650) 969-8901.

Chapter 5   Kindling Kinship
1. Patricia Sellers, "What Exactly Is Charisma?" *Fortune*, January 1996, 74.
2. Mary Oliver, "Mockingbirds," *Atlantic Monthly*, February 1994.

Part 3   Accepting—Creating a Safe Haven for Risk Taking
1. Sidney Jourard, *The Transparent Self: Self-Disclosure and Well-Being* (New York: Van Nostrand Reinhold, 1971).
2. John Powell, *Why Am I Afraid to Tell You Who I Am?*, rev. ed. (Allen, TX: Tabor, 1990), 12.

Chapter 11   Socrates' Great Secret

1. Pierce J. Howard, *The Owner's Manual for the Brain: Everyday Applications from Mind-Brain Research* (Austin, TX: Leornian Press, 1994), 180.
2. Gerard R. Roche, "Much Ado about Mentors," *Harvard Business Review*, January 1979.

Chapter 17   Linking Proficiency to Purpose

1. Jack Stack, *The Great Game of Business* (New York: Doubleday, 1992), 186.

Chapter 19   Inviting Your Protégé to Enchantment

1. Adam Smith, *Powers of Mind* (New York: Ballantine Books, 1978), 85.
2. Aldous Huxley, *The Doors of Perception* (New York: Harper, 1954).

Chapter 26   Arduous Alliances

1. Albert Mehrabian, *Silent Messages: Implicit Communication of Emotions and Attitudes* (Belmont, CA: Wadsworth, 1981), 12.

Bibliography

Barbian, Jeff. "The Road Best Traveled." *Training*, May 2002.

Bell, Chip R., and Bilijack R. Bell. *Magnetic Service: Secrets for Creating Passionately Devoted Customers*. San Francisco: Berrett-Koehler, 2003.

Bell, Chip R., and John R. Patterson. *Take Their Breath Away: How Imaginative Service Creates Devoted Customers*. Hoboken, New Jersey: Wiley, 2009.

Bell, Chip R., and John R. Patterson. *Wired and Dangerous: How Your Customers Have Changed and What to Do about It*. San Francisco: Berrett-Koehler, 2011.

Bell, Chip R., and Heather Shea. *Dance Lessons: Six Steps to Great Partnerships in Business & Life*. San Francisco: Berrett-Koehler, 1998.

Bell, Chip R., and Ron Zemke. *Managing Knock Your Socks Off Service*. 3rd ed. New York: AMACOM, 2013.

Castaneda, Carlos. *The Teachings of Don Juan: A Yaqui Way of Knowledge*. Berkeley: University of California Press, 1968.

Connellan, Thomas K. *How to Grow People into Self-Starters*. Ann Arbor: The Achievement Institute, 1991.

Connellan, Thomas K. *Bringing Out the Best in Others*! Three Keys for Business Leaders, Educators, Coaches and Parents. Austin, TX: Bard Press, 2003.

Dass, Ram (Richard Alpert). *The Only Dance There Is*. Garden City, NY: Anchor Press, 1974.

de Geus, Arie. *The Living Company: Habits for Survival in a Turbulent Business Environment*. Boston: Havard Business School Press, 1997.

De Pree, Max. *Leadership Jazz*. New York: Doubleday, 1992.

Easton, Nina. "Guide to the Future." *Fortune Magazine*, January 16, 2012.

Edvinsson, Leif, and Michael S. Malone. *Intellectual Capital: Realizing Your Company's True Value by Finding Its Hidden Roots.* New York: HarperBusiness, 1997.

"Emerging Work Force Study." *Business Week,* March 1, 1999.

Fishman, Charles. "The War for Talent." *Fast Company,* August 1998.

Goldsmith, Marshall. *What Got You Here Won't Get You There.* New York: Hyperion Books, 2007.

Goldsmith, Marshall. *Mojo: How to Get It, How to Keep It, How to Get It Back If You Lose It.* New York: Hyperion Books, 2009.

Goldsmith, Marshall, Beverly Kaye, and Ken Shelton, eds. *Learn Like a Leader: Today's Top Leaders Share Their Learning Journeys.* Boston: Nicholas Brealey Publishing, 2010.

Goldsmith, Marshall, Laurence S. Lyons, and Alyssa Freas, eds. *Coaching for Leadership: How the World's Greatest Coaches Help Leaders Learn.* San Francisco: Jossey-Bass, 2000.

Goldsmith, Marshall, Larraine Segil, and James Belasco, eds. *Partnering: The New Face of Leadership.* New York: AMACOM, 2003.

Greenleaf, Robert K. *Servant Leadership: A Journey into the Nature of Legitimate Power and Greatness.* New York: Paulist Press, 1977.

Howard, Pierce J. *The Owner's Manual for the Brain: Everyday Applications from Mind-Brain Research.* Austin: Leornian Press, 1994.

Huxley, Aldous. *The Doors of Perception.* New York: Harper, 1954.

Jourard, Sidney. *The Transparent Self: Self-Disclosure and Well-Being.* New York: Van Nostrand Reinhold, 1971.

Kawasaki, Guy. *Enchantment: The Art of Changing Hearts, Minds, and Action.* New York: Penguin, 2011.

Kaye, Beverly, and Julie Winkle Giulioni. *Help Them Grow or Watch Them Go: Career Conversations Employees Want.* San Francisco: Berrett-Koehler, 2012.

Knowles, Malcolm. *The Adult Learner: A Neglected Species.* 4th ed. Houston: Gulf Publishing, 1990.

Kouzes, James M., and Barry Z. Posner. *Credibility: How Leaders Gain and Lose It, Why People Demand It.* San Francisco: Jossey-Bass, 1993.

Kouzes, James M., and Barry Z. Posner. *The Leadership Challenge.* San Francisco: Jossey-Bass, 1995.

Kram, Kathy E. "Phases of the Mentor Relationship." *Academy of Management Journal* 26, no. 4 (1983): 608–625.

Lane, Tom, and Alan Green. *The Way of Quality: Dialogues on Kaizen Thinking.* Austin: Dialogos Press, 1994.

Leonard-Barton, Dorothy. *Wellsprings of Knowledge: Building and Sustaining the Sources of Innovation.* Boston: Harvard Business School Press, 1995.

Mackay, Harvey B. . *Swim with the Sharks without Being Eaten Alive: Outsell, Outmanage, Outmotivate, and Outnegotiate Your Competition.* New York: Morrow, 1988.

Margolis, Fredric H., and Chip R. Bell. *Instructing for Results: Managing the Learning Process.* San Diego: Pfeiffer and Co., 1986.

Mehrabian, Albert. *Silent Messages: Implicit Communication of Emotions and Attitudes.* Belmont, CA: Wadsworth, 1981.

Murray, Margo. *Beyond the Myths and Magic of Mentoring: How To Facilitate an Effective Mentoring Process.* San Francisco: Jossey-Bass, 1991.

Oliver, Mary. "Mockingbirds." *Atlantic Monthly,* February 1994.

O'Toole, James. *Leading Change: Overcoming the Ideology of Comfort and the Tyranny of Custom.* San Francisco: Jossey-Bass, 1995.

Powell, John. *Why Am I Afraid to Tell You Who I Am?* Rev. ed. Allen, TX: Tabor, 1990.

Ricks, Thomas E. "What Ever Happened to Accountability?" *Harvard Business Review,* October 2012.

Roche, Gerald R. "Much Ado about Mentors." *Harvard Business Review,* January 1979.

Rogers, Carl R. *On Becoming a Person: A Therapist's View of Psychotherapy.* Boston: Houghton Mifflin, 1961.

Saint-Exupéry, Antoine. *The Little Prince.* New York: Harcourt, Brace and World, 1943.

Sellers, Patricia. "What Exactly Is Charisma?" *Fortune,* January 1996.

Senge, Peter M. *The Fifth Discipline: The Art and Practice of the Learning Organization.* New York: Doubleday, 1990.

Showkeir, Jamie, and Maren Showkeir. *Authentic Conversations: Moving From Manipulation to Truth and Commitment.* San Francisco: Berrett-Koehler, 2008.

Smith, Adam. *Powers of Mind.* New York: Ballantine Books, 1978.

Stack, Jack. *The Great Game of Business.* New York: Doubleday, 1992.

Stolzfus, Tony. *Coaching Questions: A Coach's Guide to Powerful Asking Skills.* Virginia Beach, VA: Tony Stolzfus, 2008.

Treasurer, Bill. *Courage Goes to Work: How To Build Backbones, Boost Performance, and Get Results*. San Francisco: Berrett-Koehler, 2008.

Vaill, Peter B. *Spirited Leading and Learning: Process Wisdom for a New Age*. San Francisco: Jossey-Bass, 1998.

Zemke, Ron, and Chip R. Bell. *Knock Your Socks Off Service Recovery*. New York: AMACOM, 2000.

Thanks

To our special publishing friends, especially Neal M., Jeevan S., Steve P., Dianne P., Mike C., Kristen F., Rick W., Maria Jesus A., Katie S., Marina C., Zoe M., Charlotte A., Seth Adam S., Sarah Jane H., Tora E., Leslie S., Detta P., and Jamie F.

To our special work friends, specifically John P. and Sarah M.

To important mentors, expressly Avis B., Ray B., Effie P., Len N., etc.

To our cherished family, particularly Nancy B., Lyda G., Lisa B., Bilijack B., Kaylee B., Annabeth B., Cassie B., Bryan G., and Kelly G.

Index

About the Authors

Michael Romeo, Jr.

Chip R. Bell is a senior partner with the Chip Bell Group and manages the office near Atlanta. He has served as consultant, trainer, or speaker to such major organizations as GE, Microsoft, State Farm, Marriott, Lockheed-Martin, Cadillac, KeyBank, Ritz-Carlton Hotels, Pfizer, Eli Lilly, USAA, Merrill Lynch, Allstate, Caterpillar, Hertz, Accenture, Verizon, Home Depot, Harley-Davidson, and Victoria's Secret. He has served as an adjunct instructor at Cornell University, Manchester University (UK), and Penn State University. Additionally, he was a highly decorated infantry unit commander in Vietnam with the elite 82nd Airborne and served on the faculty of the Instructional Methods Division of the Army Infantry School.

Chip is the author of nineteen books, including *Wired and Dangerous* (co-authored with John Patterson and a winner of a 2011 Axiom Award as well as a 2012 Independent Publishers IPPY Award), *Take Their Breath Away* (also with John Patterson), *Instructing for Results (*with Fredric Margolis*)*, *Magnetic Service* (with Bilijack Bell and winner of the 2004 Benjamin Franklin Award), *Managing Knock Your Socks Off Service* (with Ron Zemke), *Service Magic* (also with Ron Zemke), and *Dance Lessons* (with Heather Shea Schultz). He has also contributed chapters to *The Sales Training Handbook, The Training and Development Handbook,* and *The Handbook of Human Resource Development.* The first edition of *Managers as Mentors* won the prestigious Athena Award for excellence in mentoring literature.

His articles on training and learning have appeared in such professional journals as *T+D, Training, HR Magazine, Personal Excellence, Workforce Training News, The Toastmaster, Educa-*

tional Leadership, Adult Training, Adult Leadership, Storyteller's Journal, and *Journal of European Training* (UK). Chip's articles on leadership and mentoring have appeared in *Leadership Excellence, MWorld, Entrepreneur, Leader to Leader, Advanced Management Journal, Sales and Service Excellence, Journal of Management Consulting, Customer Relationship Management, Quality Digest, Staff Digest,* and *Today's Leaders.*

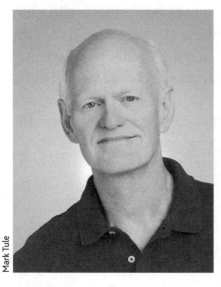

Marshall Goldsmith was recently recognized as the number 1 leadership thinker in the world and the number 7 business thinker in the world at the biannual Thinkers50 ceremony sponsored by the *Harvard Business Review.* He is the million-selling author or editor of thirty-one books, including the *New York Times* and *Wall Street Journal* bestsellers *MOJO* and *What Got You Here Won't Get You There*—a *WSJ* #1 business book and winner of the Harold Longman Award for Business Book of the Year. His books have been translated into twenty-eight languages and become bestsellers in eight countries.

Marshall's professional acknowledgments include Institute for Management Studies—Lifetime Achievement Award (one of only two ever awarded); American Management Association—fifty great thinkers and leaders who have influenced the field of management over the past eighty years; *BusinessWeek*—fifty great leaders in America; *Wall Street Journal*—top ten executive educators; *Forbes*—five most-respected executive coaches; *Leadership Excellence*—top five thinkers on leadership; *Economic Times* (India)—top CEO coaches of America; *Economist* (UK)—most credible executive advisors in the new era of business; National Academy of Human Resources—Fellow of the Academy (America's top HR award); World HRD Congress—2011 global leader in HR thinking; 2011 Tata Award (India) for Global HR Excellence; *Fast Company*—America's preeminent executive coach; and Leader to Leader Institute—2010 Leader of the Future Award.

Dr. Goldsmith's Ph.D is from UCLA's Anderson School of Management. He teaches executive education at Dartmouth's Tuck School and frequently speaks at leading business schools. Marshall's other books include *Succession: Are You Ready?*, a *WSJ* bestseller; *The Leader of the Future*, a *BusinessWeek* bestseller; and the *AMA Handbook of Leadership*, *The Organization of the Future 2*, and *The Leadership Investment*, all three of which are American Library Association-Choice award winners for academic business books of the year.

How Can We Help?

We do keynotes and workshops on mentoring and coaching. Let us know if either is needed to assist in meeting the learning goals of your organization. We also enjoy providing consultation on leadership mentoring and executive coaching.

We encourage you to visit our individual websites and follow our blogs on www.managersasmentors.com.

Chip R. Bell
Phone: (214) 522-5777
Email: chip@chipbell.com
Website: www.chipbell.com
Blog site: www.managersasmentors.com.

Marshall Goldsmith
Phone: 858-759-0950
Email: marshall@marshallgoldsmith.com
Website: www.marshallgoldsmith.com
Blog site: marshallgoldsmith.blogspot.com

Also by Chip Bell

Chip R. Bell and John Patterson

Wired and Dangerous
How Your Customers Have Changed and to Do About It

Customers today are picky, fickle, vocal, and "all about me" vain. With the reach and influence of the Internet, they are also powerful. Chip Bell and John Patterson analyze this service revolution and, using real-world examples, provide a tested formula for transforming today's edgy customers into eager partners.

Paperback, 264 pages, ISBN 978-1-60509-975-0
PDF ebook, ISBN 978-1-60509-976-7

Chip R. Bell and Bilijack R. Bell

Magnetic Service
Secrets for Creating Passionately Devoted Customers

Do you long to build a cult-like following for your business? Would you like to have customers who don't just recommend you but assertively insist that their friends do business with you? Discover the seven "magnetic service" secrets that have created devoted fans for brands such as Starbucks, Harley-Davidson, and the Ritz-Carlton.

Paperback, 192 pages, ISBN 978-1-57675-375-0
PDF ebook, ISBN 978-1-60509-642-1

Berrett–Koehler Publishers, Inc.
www.bkconnection.com

800.929.2929

Chip R. Bell and Heather Shea

Dance Lessons
Six Steps to Great Partnerships in Business and Life

This comprehensive guide to building partnerships with passion, quality, heart, and soul features exciting tools for selecting the right form of partnership, smart ways to accurately pick good partners, effective methods for dealing with difficult partners and partnerships, vital cues that tell you when a partnership is ready to end, helpful tips on how to end it, and more!

Hardcover, 240 pages, ISBN 978-1-57675-043-8
PDF ebook, ISBN 978-1-60994-150-5

Chip R. Bell

Customers as Partners
Building Relationships That Last

Customers as Partners examines the qualities that form the core of all lasting relationships and describes a way of business where personal interactions, not simply sales, take center stage. When you put the relationship first, customers and clients will respond in kind and will feel they have a personal stake in your success.

Hardcover, 256 pages, ISBN 978-1-881052-54-8

Berrett–Koehler Publishers, Inc.
www.bkconnection.com

800.929.2929